WE LIVE AND MOVE AND HAVE OUR BEING

For, 'In him we live and move and have our being.'

Acts 17:28

"The Christian mind sees human life and human history
Held in the hands of God
And there is nothing in daily life and thought,
However supposedly trivial,
That can be dismissed as being outside
The scope of that scrutiny which separates
Obedience from disobedience
Good from evil"

Assessing the Christian 'mind' of C. S. Lewis, "Pilgrim's Guide" Wm. B Eerdmans, 1998

First Edition – September 2012

ISBN
978-1-4602-0316-3 (Paperback)

Published by:

FriesenPress
Suite 300 – 852 Fort Street
Victoria, BC, Canada V8W 1H8

www.friesenpress.com

Distributed to the trade by The Ingram Book Company

For family and friends,
Children and grandchildren
And those to come

Table of Contents

The Prairie Home

Manitoba skies are generally blue. The skies are big, very big. Clouds are what make the sky look different from time to time, but cold, warm or hot the skies are blue. I remember the skies most of all when my memory began. If, on a warm summer morning, I woke up from a long sleep, it was a pleasant thing to wander down the path to the outhouse in my flour-sack shift, stop by the sandbox and meander back to the house under the blue umbrella of warm sky to find breakfast waiting. The blue sky gives you a lot of freedom when you are little. In some recess of your consciousness you know that you have to stay connected to the familiar things in your life. Oh, you can wander here and there on the flat earth, but you will always be tethered to the house, the barn, the garden, the swamp and the windbreak that corrals your familiar world, but up above is that infinite, expansive, unbelievable canopy of sky that gives the flat earth a dimension of eternity.

Why was I born in Manitoba? Manitoba was the place of refuge for my father's family who had narrowly escaped the horrors of Russia in 1925. Fortunately, his family had the courage to leave their village in Siberia because of the unrest, famine and political terror that followed the communist revolution. Living in the village of Gnadenheim, District of Slavgorod (Redkaja Dubrowa) in Siberia for thirteen years of his life, my father in his personal memoir refers to the period from 1912 to 1925 as the best years of his life. His family had left the village of Alexandertahl in the Molotschna in the Ukraine in 1912. This part of Siberia was then virgin territory, which opened for settlement in 1908. My father describes his life from age six to age nineteen in these memoirs and it is apparent that his life was prosperous and satisfying.

My mother's family lived in the same village and by the time her family left Russia in October, 1925, my parents had already fallen in love but their opportunity to marry did not arise until two years later in Canada They were married on July 24th, 1927 in Osborne, Manitoba. My mother's name was Helena Wedel and her father; Jacob Wedel was the village schoolteacher in Gnadenheim, who taught both mother and father. They attended the same Mennonite Brethren Church and enjoyed village activities and the social life in the village.

The Canadian Mennonite Board of Colonization's record of my father's family's entry into Manitoba includes a short history of leaving Moscow on August 20th, 1925, arriving in (Riga) Rezekne, Latvia on August 25th, 1925, leaving (Riga) Rezekne on August 27th, arriving in Rotterdam and departing from Rotterdam on the steamship Leerdam for Mexico. Grandfather Peter Suderman, in his memoirs indicates a stay of four days in Riga, then travel by train to Berlin and then to Rotterdam where they had a stay of 13 days before embarking on the Leerdam. There was a further stop in Antwerp and then five stops in Spain. Before landing in Veracruz, Mexico, three days were spent in Havana, Cuba. Mexico was a disappointment for my father's family. They were taken to Irapuato, which was reasonable in prospect, but unsuitable for his family's future as grandfather Suderman wrote in his short summary of his life. He immediately contacted the Canadian Mennonite Board of Colonization in Rosthern, Saskatchewan and applied for entry to Canada, arriving in Canada at the Emerson, Manitoba entry point on January 25, 1926.

My father to the end of his days, spoke with great delight of his opportunity to have what he considered a world cruise when he was nineteen years of age, which age allowed him the privilege of spending time sightseeing in the stop-over cities. Father and his younger brother were given the freedom to see the cities on their own during the stopovers.

The adventure to Mexico was a mistake. Apparently the Mexican agent, who had solicited emigrants in their village, had been successful in persuading the prospective immigrants that warm Mexico was infinitely preferable to cold Canada. My father, knowing that my mother's family was intending to immigrate to Canada, had already resolved to make his way to Canada at the earliest opportunity and to his relief, the whole family made the decision to make Canada their home.

Manitoba does not always have blue skies, but mostly it does. During their first years in Manitoba, my father's family lived in Osborne. In the year 1926, the harvest stood in fields of water, with little harvested. The spring of 1927 was so cold and wet that no seeding was possible until early June. That late seeding accomplished, July 27th saw the wedding of my parents, John and Helena who then shared the household with father's parents. Again, rain prevented any harvest and the grain rotted in the fields. In desperation, the family worked as wage earners in 1928 and in 1929. To add to the hardship and distress, grandmother Helena Suderman suffered a stroke and died on May 15th, 1929. My grandfather was distraught and sought to ease his pain by marrying Helena's younger sister within three months, on July 14th, 1929.

My parents having married on July 24, 1927 began to look for opportunities to purchase their own farm. An Agreement for Sale (in the German language) was entered into by my father together with his brother-in-law, Jacob Wedel, for 640 acres for the price of $23,700.00 with interest at 5.5 % on January the 1st, 1929. The document showed that the sum of $ 7,500.00 was owed to a John McKenzie of Vancouver and provision was made that payment could be made directly to John McKenzie if the vendor, Robert R. Whiting failed to discharge this obligation.

The property was approximately four miles south of the town of Wawanesa, the town is notable in Canadian history in that the first Mutual Insurance Company in Canada was incorporated here. The town is on the Souris River. The chattels and stock that came with the farm were itemized in the contract and included 13 horses and harnesses for 12 horses, 4 cows, 3 sows, 2 ploughs, 1 rake, 1 drill, 2 binders, 1 cultivator, 1 disk, 2 box wagons, 2 racks, 1 grass machine, 1 horse drawn rake, 1 sled, some yard tools, 750 bushels of feed, 100 bushels of seed barley, 300 bushels of seed oats, 150 bushels of seed wheat.

Fences and barbed wire were the markers of your domain. The uncultivated edges along the fence allow some of the traditional prairie grasses to assert themselves. These strips provide an interesting resource for curious children in contrast to the ploughed and seeded fields. On each side of the full section, dirt roads provided access to neighbouring farms.

The family farm was a full section of more or less flat black earth of arable land suitable for growing wheat and other grains. A wandering shallow dry creek bed dissected the square land mass. This creek bed provided the cow path to the distant pasture. Various clumps of trees provided hidden refuge for small and large animals in the pasture. The low areas in the pasture permitted clusters of trees and shrubs to develop some permanence. The pasture was crowned by a low hill, which was a good vantage point from which to view the whole farm. Prairie wild flowers were pungent and reliable. The tall clover with white blossoms has the most arresting and charming fragrance of all the wild grasses. We were always excited when we spotted the vivid orange of the tiger lily.

It is amazing how many details are etched in my memory of this farm. The base of the large hip-roofed barn was made of large stones with masonry to hold them together. Above the base, the wooden structure towered two stories. The ample loft held the hay and straw for the animal's winterfeed. The barn was always populated with at least a dozen cats or more. Cats were never invited into our house. The barn usually had a dozen horses and as many or more cows and beef cattle. On the walls hung the saddles, harnesses and the other necessary farm accoutrements. Our first dog was Rover who gave little Peter a bite on his cheek and forehead when Peter ventured too close as the dog was lapping up his milk and foam. The dog was banished to live with our neighbours.

Scattered here and there were other farm buildings. Granaries, equipment sheds, a pig sty and, significantly, chicken coops as well as a turkey pen. Straw stacks and hay piles rounded out the landscape. Straw stacks and hay piles were amazing encouragements to play hide and seek and were most adaptable as slides. We had few if any toys.

Our house was protected on its western and northern sides by Caragana trees planted as a double windbreak. The house was a simple two-story structure constructed of wood. I do not remember the inside clearly. It was relatively small for our large family, especially when Uncle Henry Suderman's family shared almost half of the house. The exterior was a weathered grey. Even the window frames were unpainted. For the winter, an insert of a glazed window frame with three little holes in the bottom of the frame with a swivel latch to allow air in when required augmented the single glazed windows. There were no plantings next to the house, just natural grasses. Not too far away from the house was the outhouse, usually somewhat discretely placed behind shrubs or trees.

Our nearest relatives were the grandparents, Suderman, who lived in Dunrea, south of our farm. Somewhat further south were the Peter and John Ratzlaff families as well as the Cornelius Klassen family. These families lived in adjoining complexes and it was here that the Mennonite community would gather occasionally for services in the summertime. Our Wedel grandparents lived even further south in a place named Margaret where an Unrau family lived as well. Almost at the US border was the town of Boissevain. Here there was a considerable group of Mennonites and a church was built in that area fairly early on. At that time, there were informal meetings in various homes, a school as a meeting place and eventually, a church building.

The winters were long and cold. Travel was by way of a Model T Ford in summer time and a horse-drawn sleigh in wintertime. Summers could be warm and lovely.

Mother, Helena (Wedel) Suderman and father, John Peter Suderman, posing shortly after they were married.

Living on the Land

The family grew and enjoyed the simple pleasures of life in the new country of Canada. We had wonderful neighbours close at hand. Mrs Raisin and her husband had no children. Mr Raisin's brother lived and farmed with them. The Raisins took it upon themselves to advise mother and father on the intricacies of the new culture they had now embraced. Mrs Raisin was usually available to assist father in the birthing of the children. Mother proudly said that Mrs Raisin insisted that she could not as much as find a dirty clothe when she came to the house to help father with the birthing. Mother was a very good housekeeper and managed infants, diapers, farm clothes, etc., using a scrub board, limited hot water, and no drying facility except hanging laundry on cords above the kitchen stove during cold or wet weather. Food was not a problem for a farm wife and not so much different than the challenges faced in Russia.

In 1937, my father became very gaunt, thin and unable to work. After months of illness, he lapsed into a coma and was rushed to the Brandon hospital where he remained in a coma for three days and nights. He was diagnosed as being diabetic and fortunately, insulin had recently been discovered by Banting and Best and was now marketed. Doctors were just beginning to prescribe it as the miracle drug for diabetics. My father returned to work on the farm. His health was poor and his prospects in doubt. In his state of despair as he was ploughing the fields with his horses, he says he heard a voice in his spirit recite a verse from Psalm 18, verse 29 " and with my God, I can leap over a wall"; the confidence of the Psalmist David provided him with the courage to accept his condition and he lived another forty-two years, giving himself insulin injections three times a day, balancing his energy output, and with the assistance of mother, keeping himself rigidly to a vegetable and protein diet.

He never suffered the usual consequences of careless diabetics such as gangrene in the lower limbs, eyesight problems, and problems with wounds that would not heal. In fact, one of the younger sisters who grew up with a diabetic father came to believe that only women and children ate sweets and white bread. She was astounded when she noticed that other men would eat “women and children’s food” as she recalled at the 50th wedding anniversary celebration of my parents. The diagnosis was later made that the diabetes was the result of a viral infection and not a hereditary disposition. None of the ten children or twenty-three grandchildren of the family has contracted diabetes. It is interesting to note that my father in the 1930’s introduced foods that are currently popular, to the family. Soy beans, flax, cod-liver were introduced as supplements to our diet and a strong emphasis on vegetables as part of father’s diet as well as our diet were mandatory in our home.

Poverty is what I never really experienced. It was obviously a part of our family’s experience, but it did not impact the way we felt. Hardship, on the other hand, is something we experienced at times in our lives. I have a vivid memory of my mother standing in the middle of our yard, surrounded by five small children. She is alone as my father is in the hospital in Brandon. She is wringing her hands and crying because two trucks are loading the seed grain from the granaries. The vendor of the farm has not been paid the required mortgage payment by my parents and as a result he is seizing the grain. Part of that memory is also of a thunderstorm that had just passed and there were lovely little puddles to splash around in. I think we, eventually a family of ten children, never felt impoverished because we were always surrounded by security and love, even in the midst of excruciating hardship.

As a result of my father's illness, his brother Henry with his wife Annie, together with her two children came to join the farm venture. Her first husband, Jacob Friesen had died of tuberculosis. This provided us with playmates and a small community, not to mention a larger school population. Before long, the mothers each gave birth to a new son, both named Peter Suderman after grandfather Peter Suderman. Family traditions trump any other consideration when it comes to naming the child. A second lean-to was added giving each family their own kitchen and entrance. Each family had two bedrooms upstairs and with time the house burgeoned with children.

The Manitoba landscape requires a kind of intimacy from small children. The smell of clover, the scent of wild roses, the grass fragrances still linger in my memory and are recalled at once if experienced again in later life. The small clusters of poplars with their secrets of owls, the swampy meadows and cow pastures, populated with the red-winged blackbirds and meadowlarks were infinitely interesting and one spent hours wandering and exploring rocky outcrops, wild strawberry patches, wildflower abundance, get lost in tall corn fields and traverse fields of waving grain. In the springtime, one knew just where to follow the barbed wire fences to find the mauve crocus to surprise not only us, but also our mother. Since mother's birthday was on June 15th, we made sure to bring her a bouquet of wild roses on her special day. The advantage of growing up in a large family is that you get a lot of warnings, but not as much supervision. You also get a lot of responsibility early in life. That results in a feeling that you are in control of your life, which serves you well for the rest of your life. We were warned to be careful when we went into the swamp, to be careful of the bull in the pasture, to be careful around strangers, and to be aware of the spring thaw and the rush of waters in the coulee.

The hired men were of dubious character in our chaste Mennonite family. They generally smoked and left smelly cigarette stubs lying about. I suppose I had never seen a naked male until I was about five and saw this hired man change his clothes in the granary where we happened to be playing on the huge mounds of grain. It was not a pretty sight, but then sex education was not a big deal when you lived on the farm, and had your cows "serviced" by a bull. Mother's breasts were there to feed the infants and aroused no particular interest whatever. Our questions about sexual activity among the animals did not always get fully answered either when we asked why the horses had those long things hanging there - which sometimes got even longer. You simply assumed some of the answers if they weren't forthcoming. You were also required to bring the cattle from the pasture, to herd the cattle on the stubble fields in the fall, riding Fanny, the white horse. During harvest, sheaves had to be stacked even though mice darted from under the grain. These chores were required of six, seven and eight year olds in our family.

The family garden was a major source of nourishment and the flowerbeds our sublime aesthetic experience. We never did have the gloriously red tulip bed that our neighbour,

Mrs. Raisin had. To this day these vivid, velvety miracles are etched in my memory and revealed the possibility of astonishing beauty coming out of the ground in springtime. Potatoes required attention, especially when they attracted what looked like ladybugs, which had to be picked off by hand – no pesticides in our generation! Potatoes were fun to dig up, especially the little nuggets. Young carrots were our favourite snack food and little green peas were worth the effort of shelling them. Lots of peas had to be picked and shelled when threshing time came around and an army of workers had to be fed. The workers seemed to be eating all the time. The fun part was to bring the in-between-time snacks out to the field in baskets. Mom was good at baking. She had this huge metal bowl, which held enough dough to bake about ten loaves at a time. Fresh bread is absolutely delicious, the crust, or cap, is the best part slathered with butter. The coffee preparation was not what we drink today. It was roasted barley and called "pripps" in the language that my parents spoke to each other.

The language is generally called "Low German" and is still spoken in northern Germany. Apparently, it was the language of commerce in the Hanseatic Trade League many years ago and survives to this day, not only in the Mennonite communities, but in Europe as well. While walking along the beach in the Canary Islands one day in about 1990, a group of people behind us were speaking in the Low German dialect to each other. My husband and I were so astonished we turned around and asked them why they were speaking that language. They said they were from Hamburg and it was in common use in that area. To us, our parents spoke the High German language, the language adopted by the Dutch speaking Mennonites during their stay in Poland after it became part of Prussia in the mid 18th Century. During this period, the Mennonites were required to give up the Dutch language in the schools and in their church services. The Low German dialect was maintained as the common vernacular. Of course, they used a few Russian words, too. One was mother's name for my father "Vang", a derivation of the Russian "Ivan" which she used most of her life.

Shoes were not readily available and rarely used in summer, so that when we went out to the grain fields we had to walk carefully among the stubble to avoid sharp stalks and other hazards. Excitement, exhaustion, noise, human and animal activity from dawn to dusk was the reality of harvest time.

As the second oldest member of my family, childcare was a given. In place of soothers, bits of cloth with sugar tucked in the middle and tied with a string were probably responsible for the sweet tooth I still have. I carry a guilty memory of dropping my baby sister Elfrieda on the front step that was a large flat rock, when she wriggled out of my small arms as I sat on the sill of the door holding her on my lap. Fortunately, her loud cries were the most alarming result.

Our mother said that she had suffered two premature births, resulting in the death of the first two sons. At one time she despaired of ever having children, which became ironic in that she had a family of ten children. She loved babies and was a fiercely loving and nurturing parent. She had the courage and stamina to cope with the physical and emotional challenges of the economic and family demands. Her hospitality was legendary among friends and relatives who had no hesitation to accept her offers to lengthy visits and overnights. Her gardens were a masterpiece and enormously productive, and many a summer evening after dinner she would tend the garden and gather the produce. Only the last two of her ten children were born in a hospital. Father was a capable midwife when other women were not available. A trip to the home of our grandparents at midnight or an evacuation to roughing it in the barn were a prelude to the announcement of a new sister or brother which we increasingly less innocent older children were able to predict.

The interesting excursions of summer included taking the grain to the elevator and stopping by the town pump to pick up drinking water. The sophistication of town was enough to pique our curiosity and it was a treat to be chosen to accompany father on one of these events. The ultimate reward of the excursion was a lollipop. The town itself was situated along the Souris River, notable for its red brick building, which housed the head office of The Wawanesa Mutual Insurance Company. Father shopped for groceries. Mother rarely left home. Other purchases were made in Brandon, thirty miles to the north or Winnipeg, one hundred and sixty miles to the east.

Brandon was the venue for the fall fair of southern Manitoba. Our experiences seemed to be limited to climbing farm machinery, especially John Deere tractors, which, painted a bright green with yellow trim and with their fine rubber tires looked so sophisticated in comparison to the old, obsolete, heavy-metal steam tractor, which sat abandoned on the farm. During the depression years, it was mostly a case of looking and longing for my father and making do with the horses. If the crop had been reasonable, we would probably have been able to wangle a Kewpie doll on a stick as a souvenir and that ultimately heavenly delicacy called a revel. On a very good day, we were given the amazing experience of a ride on the carousel. Father was subsequently inspired to make a four-armed carousel out of two beams stuck on to a mechanism that allowed it to rotate. Unfortunately, the family gene of motion sickness played havoc with this invention as we all turned green very quickly and abandoned the new contraption. It also had a fatal design flaw in that any unaware child entering the path of the moving arms was clobbered if not decapitated.

Winnipeg was the magic city that we rarely visited. It was very difficult to cope with the sensory overload that we experienced when we saw its exotic buildings, paved roads, smooth sidewalks and expansive stores. Even coming into the home of an uncle and aunt and seeing the table set with beautiful china was an aesthetic experience of indescribable proportions. Then there were the aunts with hair that waved in parallel rows and clothing that flowed and shimmered as they walked. These aunts were employed as domestic help at the prosperous white Anglo Saxon city homes and soon adopted the styles and clothing of the culture in which they found themselves.

Shopping was an experience of impossible options. Having saved the sum of one dollar over a period of two years, my sister and I had the difficult task of choosing our heart's desire and after having perused the Eaton's catalogue exhaustively at our leisure at home, we now saw the options in clear reality and the choice was momentous. My sister and I had desired the "Eaton's Beauty" doll for so long, there could be no other choice. Luella had to have the doll with the brunette hair, brown eyes and the yellow dress. I had to have the doll with the blond hair, blue eyes and blue dress. A curious fact of my life is that I married a man with very blue eyes and blond hair and my four children are all fair as are most of the grandchildren. It might be that this is only significant because I have become accustomed to the kinds of things psychologists suggest –my husband being a psychologist, conditioning is what they call these phenomena, I think.

The occasion warranted a formal photograph at a studio. Mother had sewn our dresses made of taffeta. We felt very fine. If we soiled these dresses, I recall that she would wash them outdoors in gasoline and then in water. We usually bought lovely patent shoes on these trips. The journey was made in our car, a Model A Ford.

John Peter Suderman and Helena Wedel Suderman with Luella Marie, Erna Suse, John Ernest and Lydia Kate. Mother was pregnant with Peter Alvin. The polka dot dress was her frequently worn maternity outfit.

Little Red School House

Tenterfield School, the usual one roomed prairie school with five large windows on one side and none on the other side so that there was room for the blackboards, was a half a mile from our farm at the crossroads of the prairie roads that laid out the four section farms. The two other buildings on the schoolyard were the outhouse and the barn. The use of the outhouse is obvious and the barn was for the horses that some of the children rode to school. The barn was painted white. The schoolhouse was the usual little red schoolhouse of legend. The reason I have this certain memory of the white barn is that one day I was putting my recent learning to good use by taking some green grass, finding that it provided an unusually good green stain and practicing my alphabet on the clean white clapboard when I was rudely challenged by some superior older students who reported my activity to the teacher. Not only did I have scrub my offensive activity off the barn, but also, I had to stay after school as punishment, an indescribable shame and blot on my record. Probably that is why I never again indulged in graffiti.

School was a kind of heaven. Of course, my father's diligence in teaching us to read and write the German Language was part of our home schooling before we even started to learn the English language, which did not interfere with the mastering of the English language. I had the great good fortune of having sister Luella, who was two years older and who took the brunt of the process of learning English, in that she took on the role of instructing her siblings in the new language. I recall how we pondered over the teacher's observation that every one should have some fresh "chair" every day. The mystery was solved when she conceded the next day that the teacher had said "air" not "chair". Not that we suffered from a lack of fresh air in our home. On very blizzardy winter nights in Manitoba, we would find light snowdrifts on our blankets in the morning; the snow had sifted through the less than tight window frames.

My sister's commitment to making sure I progressed as smoothly as possible in my education got her into the difficult ethical dilemma of involving us in "cheating", something we were appalled by and was certainly not in our usual repertoire. In her eagerness to help me, she mouthed the letters to me as the teacher dictated my spelling list. Fortunately, the teacher's reaction was a kind admonition that it was important that I be given an opportunity to learn without so much help.

Everything about school was exciting. In a one-room schoolhouse, entertainment as well as learning goes on all day at different levels and a huge variety of subjects. Our teachers were "Wasps" from Winnipeg or Toronto with names like Bailey and Richardson. The curriculum was as English as possible, English history and geography, English literature, English songs and a very English attitude and cultural overtone prevailed. When I first visited England years later, I had a distinct experience of deja vu, a familiar feeling that I have been here before, that I know and have experienced this landscape in the past. Being in such a dominant English culture, we had the advantage of learning the language without the usual ethnic accent component. Since Wawanesa was not like the Mennonite cultural enclaves of the East Reserve and the West Reserve in Manitoba where many villages were predominantly populated with Mennonites of both the 1875 and the 1920's immigration; it was only our home culture and the school culture that influenced our growing up years.

Since the one teacher had many different classes to teach, we worked on our own most of the time. Billy Gullett was my only classmate over a period of three and a half years. Our enrolment varied from fifteen to twenty students in all grades with one or two students in each of the grades from one to twelve. This situation gave me a lot of time to indulge in my favourite activities, reading and drawing. By the time we left for British Columbia in late October of 1941, I had read every book in the library, which was reasonable, but limited and included all grade levels. The transition to the North Poplar School on Clearbrook Road was traumatic for me in its utter boredom. Everyone did the same number of division or multiplication problems in the grade four class whether you needed the practice or not. And nothing interesting was going on in the classroom. To add insult to injury, our family name of Suderman became Superman on the play ground and most embarrassing of all; some of the many Mennonite classmates spoke the German language to each other at recess while others spoke with a heavy accent.

Manitoba winters are cold; nonetheless they presented vivid experiences of cutting big blocks of snow on a Sunday afternoon to throw into a huge vat on the stove in order to have soft water for the family wash on Monday. Huge hard drifts were excellent for running and playing on. Indian leather moccasins were the perfect footwear for the snow. Covered with a pair of rubber slip-ons when the snow became slushy, nothing provided greater comfort. The winter ice on the pond near the barn was wonderful for sleighs. The barn with warm animals was another interesting diversion with its dozen or so cats, especially at milking time when they got the foam from the top of the pail scooped into their dishes. The dead horse pulled onto the manure pile with its frozen feet sticking straight up into the sky vividly illustrated the issue of death's stark reality. Warm animal smells gave an experience of contrast to the crisp cold of the outdoors and the human and cooking aromas in the house. Hours of amusement indoors could be had from chairs and furniture turned upside down, covered with blankets to create secret hiding places and imaginary worlds.

Terror best describes the experience of a chimney fire. The ominous roar up the pipes, the red-hot smouldering and the frantic slapping of wet sacks against the pipes, which reached through the ceiling, through the bedrooms into the chimney, is indelibly etched in my mind. A failure to control the fire led to the burning down of the house, a not infrequent happening on the prairies. Such an event usually happened during a blizzard when the kitchen stove was being stoked to its limit with firewood and the howling wind drew the hot air up the flues. The bleak alternative of being homeless was unthinkable. The crisis past and the family collapsed into grateful thanksgiving.

When I saw the movie, Dr. Zhivago, I found it easy to vicariously enjoy the sleigh rides. We had such rides as children. Swathed in blankets with rocks heated in the oven at our feet we rode through the cold winter landscape on visits to our grandparents. The team of horses exuded a stream of steam as their harness jangled. The sleigh squeaked and swished over snow and frozen ponds and streams. Roads were of no importance as long as fences did not impede our progress. Springtime provided high drama and danger with its overnight thaws. One unforgettable recollection is the return home after an overnight stay. The sleigh and horses broke through the ice. The women and children were all screaming and the horses neighed and reared in terror. Somehow father and Uncle Henry managed to cross to the nearby shore on the broken ice shallows but with some water managing to seep into the sleigh and soaking our feet and blankets.

In the summertime, the double row of caragana trees that formed the windbreak for the house and garden provided adventures and intrigues. Hide and go seek was a favourite game. We loved to play "house". The older sisters cajoled younger brothers to participate. The sisters dominated by their numbers in the older part of the family even though there were six brothers and four sisters when the count was complete.

A one-horse buggy was my grandmother Maria Wedel's favourite mode of transportation in the summer. It was a delight when she would add such an excursion to our week of holiday with her in the summer time. Such a ride was very pleasant. A quick stepping horse, a warm breeze swishing past your ears and through your hair and the ultimate reward at the store – candy!

The melancholy influence of Wilf Carter, the authentic Canadian cowboy singer was my Uncle Henry's "Canadian Idol". Henry would grab his guitar and accompany us on our explorations of the coulees nearby. We were looking for chokecherries and wild blueberries, even wild plums. He would sit near by and sing and yodel much to our amusement. Though we had a radio, we had never heard of Wilf Carter. The radio in our home was the bearer of solemn news. When father came in from his work, he sat down at the table and listened to the news on CBC. This meant we had to be quiet, to stop our bickering, our laughter and our noisy ways. Occasionally, we accidentally heard some opera on Saturday. My mother opined that the coloratura soprano must surely be "verueckt" (gone mad) when she soared to the high notes at full throat. Our repertoire ranged between folk songs and hymns. The other ethereal voice that came into our home on Sunday was Charles E. Fuller. His Christian radio program put the hymn, "T'is so Sweet to Trust in Jesus" indelibly into my memory.

God was up above the blue sky. That dark night sky with the myriad stars created a mysterious up there that was surely where God was. One could never expect to see him. During cold winter nights, the aurora borealis spanned the night sky with colour that moved, changed and terrified. Majesty was the word that described his infinite qualities. God was so wholly other, no child could grasp his person, but somehow we experienced his presence daily. The conversations of the elders constantly reminded us that God had been available to them in their flight from Russia. God was spoken to daily in morning and evening prayers. Scriptures were part of the morning grace. We stood to say grace at every meal, the proper way to honour God. In every hardship, his presence was an absolute necessity.

Children in our home said their nightly prayers, the little ones simple ones:

Lieber Heiland , mach mich fromm
Dass ich in den Himmel komm

The older ones, prayers with more theological content:

Christi Blut und Gerechtigkeit
Dass ist mein Shmuck und Ehrenkleid
Damit will ich vor Gott bestehn
Wenn ich zum Himmel werd eingehen.

As we got older, even though it was challenging to disclose one's soul in extemporaneous prayer at evening devotions, especially to unforgiving siblings, there was no wiggle room.

The scattered families in our part of Manitoba had no church in which to worship for at least a decade. The simple option was a house church or even a barn church in summertime, especially to celebrate weddings. Some well-meaning adult would gather the children into a bedroom to teach a Sunday school class. A beautiful scripture card with a Hans Duerer etching of Biblical figures would be a treasured memento to take home. The weeks that it survived would allow for ample time to ponder the angelic beings and other worldly representations. To a child somewhat deprived of sensory experiences, such visible renderings were a source of knowledge and mystery at the same time.

Father had always been interested in chickens. When I was very young, I recollect a small machine heated by coal oil lamps in our pantry in which he put eggs and lo and behold, after 30 days baby chicks emerged, just as if the mother hen was no longer needed. He eventually set up a business of hatching chickens commercially when we moved to British Columbia. In Manitoba, the work on the farm was growing grains and raising livestock. The severe weather became a burden for father and with many family members moving to British Columbia, words about the paradise in the west brought us to the Fraser Valley in October of 1941.

Imagination is what creates marvellous dreams when knowledge of reality is not there. In my mind's eye the Rocky Mountains, which we would have to cross before we reached the Promised Land of British Columbia were mighty triangles that reached into the sky and which we would have to ascend from the east and descend on the western side. I shivered in anticipation of this brave event when we would merely open the car windows, reach out and touch the clouds.

Reality proved to be somewhat different, but spectacular nonetheless. Our 1939 Ford pulled a trailer without its own brakes, which was loaded with furniture and belongings we could not be without. Upon reaching Saskatchewan, we had crossed into the United States in order to avoid the Trans-Canada Highway and benefit from the more developed American road system. Late on a Saturday night we were descending the tortuous mountain highway into Helena, Idaho, when the tires began to smoke from the overuse of the brakes and the push of the trailer on the car. One of the headlights had fallen out during the day and so the one-eyed monster, our Model A Ford roared down the mountain road, curve after curve to the agonized prayers of my mother and the now silent clutch of children and the anxious mutterings of my father. Mercifully we arrived at the foot of the last decline, pulled into a garage where attendants quickly poured buckets of water on the smoking tires and the seven children and the parents evacuated the car in a flash.

A visit to Grandfather Peter Suderman and step-grandmother Susie was made to Rosthern, Saskatchewan as part of the trip. They had moved to Saskatchewan several years earlier. The children of grandfather's second family, were Erna, the same age as Luella, Victor, who was my age and

Abe, who was my brother John's age. The connection with grandfather's older children had become somewhat strained and was only resolved in later life. Grandfather's hasty marriage to his first wife's sister who was twenty years younger than he had put a rift in the family. My grandfather was a very gentle person. I remember his sonorous voice most of all. My recollection is not just the timbre of his voice but also the memory of grandfather reading. I never saw my grandfather again after we moved to British Columbia, so it has become a treasured memory.

When we left Manitoba, there were nine of us; the parents and seven children in a Model A Ford car. Jacob Victor was just over a year old. Mother says he bounced on her lap all the way to British Columbia and the only respite she had was when he was sleeping, also on her lap. In the back were the other five children. John was allowed to travel with Uncle Henry and Aunt Annie in their car as their family had only three children at that point. My recollection of this most unpleasant journey had to do with my proneness to motion sickness that prevented me from enjoying any food on this trip except for drinks and the occasional fruit. I lay on the backseat while the other children sat on the edge of the seat in front of me. The motels we stayed in barely accommodated us.

Here is a brief summary of the family that left for British Columbia in October of 1941:

Luella, as the oldest member of the family, took the injunctions seriously to be an example to the other children.

As the second child in a growing family, I became second in command in assisting mother. To distinguish me from my

Aunt Erna, I was frequently referred to as "Unsere Erna" which gave a strong sense of belonging.

John was called "Sonny" when he was small for two reasons. The first was that he smiled a lot and the second was that he was the first son.

Lydia was born with hair that required an immediate haircut. She was small and agile and walked early. She was referred to as "Die kleine Puppe".

Peter came next. He is known for his wry sense of humour. Rover, our family dog left the unfortunate scar on his face.

Elfrieda was the last of the girls had an easy laugh and a friendly disposition and had the advantage of having the best hair that was usually braided into French braids.

Jack was the last of the children born in Manitoba and he was a sturdy child. This is the family that arrived in British Columbia in October of 1941.

Father regained his health and learned how to cope with his diabetes. Mother is holding Jack (Jacob) with Elfrieda taken in the summer of 1940. The family left for British Columbia in October of 1941.

The Rain Forest

The moist undergrowth smelling of decay, the green cedars, firs and hemlock interspersed with alder and poplars were the predominant features of the landscape on Clearbrook Road in Abbotsford where our new home was located.

The logging crews had not too recently finished their plunder of the first growth forest and their debris of cable, cooking and camp discards littered the open spaces. Former rail spurs left criss-crossing trails among the new growth and the enormous stumps stood as defeated witnesses to the rape of the forest. These stumps provided the new conquerors of this land (our family) with a huge challenge. Dynamite was the weapon of choice and the huge brutish bulldozers were the tanks in this war on the landscape. Instead of wheat sheaves, we children now lugged dismembered roots and branches to the huge bonfires lighting up the skies on a summer evening. During rain, they became sullen heaps of smoking debris. The earth was brown and full of organic materials, not like the black soil of Manitoba. Bracken, fern, huckleberry, salal bushes, and prickly Oregon berry were new acquaintances. Mountains reared up in every direction and the rolling landscape left little room for the often-gray skies and creeping fog.

A snug little cottage with roses climbing over the veranda roof was our first home. The exterior was finished with hand-hewn cedar shakes Fir trees surrounded all the buildings on the 30-acre farm my parents purchased on Clearbrook Road. There was a root cellar with apples tucked into sand.

There was a small barn built mainly with six-foot lengths of hand split cedar for cows and livestock, but no horses. Most importantly for father, there was a chicken barn for two hundred hens. My father's choice was to be a poultry farmer and his ambition was to set up a chick hatchery. This decision was central to our life then and more so to the family's life for the next thirty-five years.

In many ways, our new life seemed idyllic. The soft climate made outdoor living more immediate. Fruit trees and productive gardens were so accessible and satisfying to young children.

Nevertheless, the first year in British Columbia became a desperate challenge to earn a livelihood, a task shared by the whole family. True, we had several cows, chickens whose eggs were sold and a good garden but that was not enough to feed and clothe the family. Mother became pregnant and had more than sufficient work to care for seven children, the oldest of which was eleven years old. Father managed to get work for one dollar an hour at the Whonnock Cedar Mill on the north side of the Fraser River.

This was the beginning of a new regime. British Columbia woke us all up to new realities. The need to earn a living became a function of the whole family. It meant that every able body was expected to pick strawberries for at least four weeks in late May and June. It meant picking raspberries in July for at least four weeks. It meant picking hops in August and September. Child labour was not an issue in those days. Farm children knew work was for everyone according to ability. We were proud of our diligence, our independence and our achievements.

This world of green and growth in British Columbia was marvelous in its productivity. The Japanese strawberry farmers were the models in the Fraser Valley. In their fields strawberry rows were productive and the wooden hullocks had to be filled carefully with berries at just the right degree of ripeness so they could be transported to the Vancouver market in optimum condition. A light dusting with a feather brush, removed any debris from the berry tips. It was a sad day when the Japanese people were dispossessed of their farms and interred in camps in the Interior of British Columbia and in Alberta.

Raspberries did not require us to crawl on the ground as we picked the ripe berries, but the stalks were covered with rasps and our hands and arms became scarred with scratches. Hops were the most detested vine to be picked because they not only exuded a green stench, but also left a thick residue of resin on our hands. It was particularly challenging for us as young teens to feel any sense of feminine beauty, especially about our hands. Our hands were stained, our arms scratched and our nails unsightly from May to September.

By the spring of 1942, I was suffering continual stomach aches, so much so that I would cringe in the ditch in pain on my way to school. In early spring of 1942, a particularly acute attack resulted in hospitalization for appendicitis. There was no health insurance available at that time and so my assurances that I was feeling well even though my temperature stayed up, resulted in my release without an operation. The reason I was determined not to suffer the indignity of an operation was because in the small fourteen bed hospital, I had witnessed a young boy being wheeled out of the operation-room in a wretched vomiting state, his hair standing up straight, his face flushed as he thrashed about.

Unfortunately, I did have a ruptured appendix by the end of July. It was precipitated by a small pail, which hung, around my stomach tied with rope as I picked raspberries. I was continually going to the bathroom hoping my stomach ache would disappear. Eventually, I was doubled-up in acute pain and rushed to the hospital at eleven o'clock on a Saturday night. Dr. Cannon had to be found and my situation was attended to in the nick of time. After the operation, I had a drain inserted into my stomach for about a month, I developed numerous adhesions because I was not required to move about for the first ten days after the operation, I had interminable nose bleeds, hacking coughs and many other discomforts, but I survived.

My memories include a bedside visit from our well-known local minister, Rev. C.C. Peters the night of the operation when my life was threatened. He arrived to pray for me having hastily dressed in the middle of the night. Of particular fascination to me were his corpulent bare feet tucked into the rubber slip-ons that are normally worn over shoes and kept from falling off his feet by some red rubber Mason jar rings. The man was genuinely caring so even in my groggy state, he was much appreciated. The outcome was also a huge hospital and doctor's bill. Another memory was that of my sister Luella walking from home to the hospital to visit me. She had lost one of the pink ribbons tied to her braids as she walked along the Trans Canada Highway. But of greatest concern to us was the wear her wartime thin canvas shoes had suffered from the walk. My pristine shoes stood neatly under the bed with relatively no wear on the thin layer of rubber but hers were showing so much wear that we were concerned they would not last the summer.

The month of August was especially hard for us. My mother was in the late stages of her pregnancy. My father was working many hours for wages in the Whonnock Cedar Mill, and my siblings were finishing picking raspberries. Henry (the eighth) was born on August 24th and I was mother's home help as I was not well enough to pick hops. For a month or more following my discharge from the hospital, I had a drain in my stomach to allow the festering wound to discharge the fluids that had festered before and after the operation. We had a pump for fresh water and even though my healing was not complete, I pumped water for the house, the chickens and the livestock.

By September, I was deemed fit to pick hops at the Canadian Hop yards. On the first day of this adventure, Luella, John and I got caught in a long line-up at the end of the day when our hops were being weighed. No one spoke for us when the bus left for home and we were abandoned. Our only solution was to walk home from the Sumas hop field to our home on Clearbrook Road. We were straggling along the Trans-Canada Highway approaching Abbotsford when the familiar sight of our model A Ford appeared in the falling darkness at about nine o'clock. On his return from work, my hysterical mother dispatched father to find us as no one in the neighborhood had any idea why we had not been on the bus. Ironically, everyone was up at five am to go to work the next day. Necessity is a hard taskmaster.

The picture records the Easter celebration in 1943. We have Easter eggs clutched in our hands. John, Jacob, Erna, Luella, Lydia, Henry, Elfrieda and Peter are enjoying the day. Uncle Peter Suderman, who was working on a dairy farm as a Conscientious Objector is visiting us from the Surrey area.

A Pacifist in Wartime

Most Mennonites who came to Canada from Russia originated in the Flemish and Dutch areas of the Netherlands as Anabaptists during the Reformation from approximately 1530 onward. They were considered heretics and suffered persecution form the Catholic as well as the Calvinists and escaped to the Dantzig and Elbing Delta area in Poland during the 16th, 17th and 18th century. Polish governments or the Prussians alternately controlled these areas. The various rulers gave refuge from persecution to the Protestant refugees.

Persecution was particularly aggressive against the Anabaptists by the Spanish Catholic Phillip of Spain who controlled Holland. The Dutch and Flemish were very desirable settlers because they had become skillful in reclaiming swampy land and turning it into productive farmland. The Mennonites became well established in the area around Dantzig and in the Elbing Werder and remained there even when Prussia took political control and introduced the German language. Up to that point, the Flemish and Dutch had retained their own languages to a large degree. A Low German dialect had also become part of their language – the language of the Hanseatic Trading League, which was the language of business for many centuries in Northern Germany, the Netherlands and the Scandinavian countries. Mennonites were forced to give up the Dutch language by the Prussian rulers but continued to use both the Low and the High German, languages. They took these languages with them in the late 18th Century to Russia and eventually to Canada. So, unfortunately, we were German-speaking immigrants in Canada during World War II.

School became a political challenge during the war. We were expected to support the "war effort". That meant showing our patriotism by purchasing war bonds. Every Friday we were asked to bring a quarter to purchase a stamp in the war bond project. After school we were to pick up all the aluminum foil from discarded wrappers along the highway to help the "war effort". The use of the German language in our community and homes effectively labeled us as being "German" which became as bad as being Japanese. Fortunately, the government had sufficient information on our origins and never subjected the Mennonites to the same treatment as the Japanese. That did not prevent many of our "English" classmates from treating us with taunts and insults. I became unhappy that I was not "English". I had suddenly become less than a Canadian – an undesirable in the land.

The Mennonite tradition of pacifism only added to the dilemma. We could not support the "war effort". We could find the cascara trees in our neighborhood from whose bark medicines for the soldiers were made and make some income by stripping the bark from the trees and getting paid for it. But we were terrified of family members being required to enlist. My uncle Peter was designated a 'conscientious objector' and was required to work on a dairy farm. Other young men were sent to do forest or park service.

My brother John had to march in drill training and learn to shoot a gun during actual target practice in grade seven. His anxiety betrayed him. His shot during target practice was nowhere near the target. Father even took us to Burns Bog to stack cut blocks of peat for a short period of time. Only recently, I discovered that this peat was vital in the production of the magnesium incendiary bomb that was dropped by the millions on European cities. Somehow, ignorance is not a sufficient answer to such a dilemma.

Pacifism is not an easy position in times of trouble. The humanist Erasmus must be given credit for promoting the peace position in the Netherlands in the early 1500's. His writings criticizing the abuses in the Catholic Church as well as the constant warfare among "Christian" princes and kingdoms in Europe. Printing had become a popular means of spreading information and so prepared the population for change and contributed to the success of Luther's Protestant movement as well as that of Menno Simons in the Netherlands. Many of the early Anabaptists suffered martyrdom for their rejection of the Catholic Church as well as their rejection of Luther and Calvin's reformation positions. The book, Martyr's Mirror reflects the horrors of persecution that many suffered. In many ways, the Mennonite people developed a sense of wandering peoplehood - always looking for the promises of living a simple life of faith and never finding a permanent promised land. Canada had become our promised land. But Mennonites have never confused the earthly and temporary 'Promised Land' with their ultimate destination, not on planet earth.

There was a small wooden church about a half a mile up the road towards the Trans-Canada Highway. It was the first regular church experience of my life. We quickly developed new friendships and a new community. The Mennonite game of sorting out connections and relationships stemming from our ancestral past became interesting. The simple non-professional, non-liturgical service participated in by the lay congregation became the model for my concept of how to do church. Several of the competent and reasonably trained men preached the sermons. Men sat on one side of the aisle, women on the other. Children sat up front so that they could be properly supervised, a strong hand on the shoulder or a tweaked ear usually had the desired effect on a chattering or unruly child. Young people sat or skulked in the balcony if they were not in the choir. For me, singing in the choir was a wonderful experience as was the congregational singing, always in four-part harmony. Public prayer participation was often profoundly emotional as many of the immigrant experiences and economic hardships continued to weigh heavily on the experience of faith of the adults who had left Russia to make a new home in Canada.

Luella, John and I made a “best friends” with Tena, Betty and John Isaak and life was exciting, particularly on Sunday afternoons when we were able to enjoy reciprocal visits. The highlight of the Sunday afternoon visits were the enjoyment of the goodies served at “Faspa”. “Faspa” is the customary light lunch served at about five pm in place of the usual supper. There were always the buns called zwiebach, cold meats, jam and lots of baked cookies and cake. The early afternoon ‘Faspa’ allowed us sufficient time to go home and do our usual chores.

The soft British Columbia weather was very different from our prairie experience. Rain was a challenge to our clothing. No fabrics were rainproof. Girls wore scarves or kerchiefs over their hair and these soaked up the rain. Our fabrics coats got soaked and even our leather shoes were always wet. There were no athletic shoes, only inexpensive leather shoes or lightweight canvas shoes made in China for the summer. We certainly didn't wear rubber boots. We had to walk to our school, about a mile and a half from home.

In grade seven, we took a circuitous bus trip to the Mt Lehman Junior School, arriving groggy and disoriented after a long morning of jolting over rough roads in a cumbersome bus. The necessity of attending school in Mt Lehman rather than in Abbotsford was partly discriminatory. It was arranged that mostly Mennonite children had to endure the long bus ride to school rather than that strictly geographic considerations were applied.

The war had taken many of the younger competent teachers out of the classrooms. My grade seven teacher was a very old spinster forced out of retirement who had long since forgotten what it meant to take command in a classroom. As a consequence, the students took over and did whatever they wished. My solution was to engage in as much time as possible in reading and artwork. I would usually have a dozen or so pictures displayed about the room.

Another specialty niche that became my domain was in cooking the school lunch. Since food was rationed during the war, the schools were obliged to provide hot lunches during the war period. Hot chocolate (a rare treat) was on Monday's menu. Tuesday saw rice pudding with raisins. Wednesday, ground beef goulash with carrots and potatoes was a hearty meal. Vanilla pudding was Thursday's specialty. We finished the week with macaroni and cheese on Friday. Cook's assistants were selected from the students who could afford to skip math or some such subject. The other criteria were that you could be depended on to stir the pot and not burn the pudding or whatever was cooking.

I qualified on one or the other and spent a lot of time in the kitchen.

Another school chore at Mt Lehman was to get drinking water from the stream close to the school. Two people were given the pail and sent out during school time. Not infrequently, this excursion took considerable time. I have always insisted that there were fresh water oysters or clams in the streams besides frogs, fingerlings and the like but to this day I have never gone back to verify my findings. Crawling around in the Mt Lehman area ravines was certainly a freedom I enjoyed.

We were fortunate to have an excellent English teacher in Grade eight by the name of Miss Lawrence. She had a commanding presence, an incisive mind and a convenient pointer to emphasize her lessons. She did not hesitate to use the pointer with excellent effect when needed. Homework became a new reality. This challenge excited me and my extensive reading in the past gave me an easy access to the intricacies of these new language considerations. Even in 1944, concern was expressed about learning standards and so in Grade eight we were given IQ tests. I must have done well, as the teachers gave me considerable affirmation after that. My full time teacher was a lovely Miss Hughes from Victoria who was very pleasant and competent.

Mt Lehman School had a woodsy acre as part of the playground. The particular subculture of students that spent its time in the woods was generally not academically inclined. One could see smoke drifting through the trees and the smell of cigarettes was evident if one wandered into the vicinity. A raunchy snatch of song, that was sung by the students trailing out of the woods perplexed me for years, but I eventually got it. No doubt it was part of my sex education, which was not a subject on the grade eight curriculums at that time. Another mystery was the reference to the French kiss. At first I wondered what the French had to do with it. Eventually I did get an explanation.

Our economic situation had improved remarkably during the war years. The production of eggs was very profitable because eggs were a food product much needed during the war years. For the same reason, father's business as a Baby Chick Hatchery did very well. The large family provided the manpower and we all became very proficient at gathering eggs and putting them in trays. The hatchery also required a lot of cleaning, stacking and boxing of the baby chicks. In addition, cultivating berries, both raspberries and strawberries kept us on our knees and in the fields.

Here are the boys in our family, John and Peter in the back, Jack and Henry in the front with young Edward sitting on the chair. Gerald was born in 1948. We were still living in our old house in 1945, but soon thereafter built a new large house. The rose bush behind the boys always flowered beautifully and we were able to wear a rose on mother's day.

Luella and I no longer wear braids- we now curled our hair. Lydia and Elfrieda are looking fine in ringlets.

The Mennonite Identity

It was at this time that the Mennonite community established the private school, the Mennonite Educational Institute in the Abbotsford area on the intersection of Clearbrook Road and Old Yale Road. Conveniently, it was only half a mile from our family farm on Clearbrook Road. My father served on the board of the school for many years. All ten children in the Suderman family graduated from the MEI. In many ways this institution set the standards for the Mennonite community in learning, culture and social interaction.

Later, sports, particularly basketball became a dominant part of the school activities. Our teachers were dedicated and competent. Academic excellence was fostered and many graduates obtained university degrees and went into the professions of medicine, law, nursing and teaching. Some of the teachers had received their education in Europe, especially in music, in the German language and in theology. Others were recent graduates of Canadian Universities. The mix served to provide us with the best of our ethnic and religious tradition as well as the excellence of the sciences and literature.

Challenges were diverse. In German literature we studied Goethe among others and memorized the epic poem "Das Lied von der Glocke". Franz Thiessen, our German instructor demanded impromptu recitation from members of the class and did not hesitate to scorn a feeble effort by a student. In English 11, Susan Krahn challenged us in creative writing assignments. My notable achievement was to use the embarrassment felt in Mr. Thiessen's class in respect to the recitation of "Das Lied von der Glocke" as the theme of my effort to imitate the piece of Stephen Leacock about his attempt to open a bank account. The fumbling and embarrassment gave me a new insight on the merit of humor.

Humor was not a particularly strong quality in my family. We were generally known as the sober Sudermans. Diligence, hard work, competence and reliability were nourished, but not humor – that was labeled as "dumheit" and could easily lead to a weakening of our moral fiber. In fact, my general demeanor was so unrelentingly unsmiling that one morning, Mr. Thiessen remarked in class, in front of all my classmates, that I probably was of the opinion that my face would crack if I smiled, much to my embarrassment and astonishment. It was the first time I had experienced an opinion of myself that I did not have of myself.

There was also a huge element of shyness in our family makeup. One of my uncles would not even wave or smile at us when he passed us in his vehicle. Whether this was just a lack of social graces or a more deep-seated problem in our family is not clear to me even today. Various cousins, aunts and uncles suffer from this syndrome in social relationships to this day.

I have very fond memories of my time at the MEI. In the yearbook of 1950 is a poem I contributed that reflects my emotional attachment.

The MEI

Last eve, as I was walking through the trees
I caught your splendor as the shadows on the hill
With rays of purple sunset mingled

Gave benediction for the close of day.
The crisp white snow thee nestled in thy charmed retreat
A quiet breeze swished gently through the trees
And shadows flitted to and fro
That deepened on the wall.
A warm light glimmering through the open door
Spoke of thy soul
Of work and cheer and faithfulness
A soul that finds its satisfaction
In work well done.
An air of greatness, courage and stability
Thou dost impart
A noble spirit called thee into being
And proudly, yet humbly thou dost stand
A symbol of a worthy cause

As a young person, you slowly discover yourself. Often what you would like to be is manifest in what you want to become as against what you are. I wanted to be some of the wonderful persons I read about. I loved to sing and one of my earliest dreams was to be a singer. I remember when I was fourteen, father asked me to help to nail on shingles on the roof of the new chicken barn. The chicken barn was a very long barn with a two story feed barn in the center. This middle barn roof was the typical hip roof barn and at the end of the day I sat on the peak and sang my heart out. My favourite songs that day were a variety of songs such as "Don't Fence Me In", Get Along Little Doggie" and the favourite chorus with the following words:

Above the clouds, that veil the blue,
Above the stars that glimmer through
There is a home unknown to care
No sorrow there for Christ is there.

I got sort of carried away and after about the tenth repetition, some rude voice in the neighboring farm shouted, “Enough already”.

As siblings, we did not learn to be encouraging to each other and my foray into voice lessons and singing of solos in the church usually resulted in them finding fault with my performance rather than giving praise. The encouragement usually came from other sources in the community and my parents. I also enjoyed creative writing. I soon learned that exposing your feelings to the world had its down side. When one of my poems was published in the yearbook, the siblings found that the surest way of taunting me was to recite my poem to me in a mocking manner.

The way to have an inner life in a large family is not to share it unless you have what Anne of Green Gables called a kindred spirit. That creates problems as well. Sister Luella, on the other hand, wished to discuss things endlessly and unfortunately, I would fall asleep on her in our shared bed and disappoint her in that area.

I was always embarrassed about my long arms, big hands and knobby knees. This embarrassment became acute in summertime as I became a teenager because of the havoc picking strawberries, raspberries and hops created on the hands. The fruits stained the fingers and the stain remained under the nails and was impervious to any kind of attempt to clean them for such events as the Sunday service. Raspberry canes are covered with small barbs and our arms would be severely scratched in spite of wearing long sleeves. Hops had the added green powder that caked the hands and fingers as you stripped the hops from the branches. This green grunge was difficult to remove and very smelly.

When we arrived in B.C. we wore braids. Occasionally our hair was wound in long strips of fabric overnight to create ringlets. I was always required to wind Lydia and Elfrieda's hair for Sunday and other events. Eventually, Luella and I were allowed to cut our hair and pin curl them with bobby pins. It was a tedious evening ritual carried out in front of the mirror in the one bathroom next to our parent's bedroom. Our parents suffered the agony of Chinese water torture as they heard the slow drip, drip, drip of the water from the tap as we painstakingly twisted our hair into curls and pinned them for the night. During the war we discovered that hair could be twisted with covered electrical wire that gave us the desired curls, especially if the hair was longer. Even our mother twisted her hair into a roll instead of the traditional bun. Eventually, home permanents gave us curls that lasted much longer.

Our social horizons were expanded significantly during the summers when we would bunk weeks at a time at various places, particularly Yarrow to pick raspberries. With people of all sorts one heard a great deal of gossip and chatter in the course of a working day in the fields. Romances among the young developed, escapades in the evenings after work were tantalizingly discussed and a sector of society was experienced that we did not usually rub shoulders with.

When I was fifteen, the most daring thing I ever did without my parent's knowledge or permission was to go to Vancouver on the B.C. Electric train that ran right through Yarrow from Chilliwack to Vancouver. It so happened that the berries were not ripe enough to pick one day. Some of our picking friends said that they had relatives in Vancouver and it was simple and inexpensive to catch the train, visit them and return at night. That is just what we did and it was pretty exciting.

The Mennonite Educational Institute, its curriculum and extra-curricular activities were central to my growing up years. We had a thorough religious education including Biblical Studies, Ethics, Catechism, and Church History. The school had excellent choirs and produced many literary events. Our academic subjects were well taught and the students achieved very well on provincial exams, garnering many scholarships on an annual basis. We wore uniforms and the general atmosphere was stimulating and nourishing. After reading the story of Marie Curie, I determined to be a scientist and took both chemistry and physics. This ambition was altered when on a visit to the University of British Columbia (UBC); I found the chemistry building to be rather arid and uninspiring. I did not win a provincial scholarship at the end of Grade 13, much to my disappointment. That meant that I had no hope of going to UBC, but would have to earn my own way through teaching. So, I took teacher training at the Provincial Normal School in 1951.

In 1948, my parents made a trip to the prairie provinces and took with them Jack, Henry, Edward and Gerald, the four youngest members of the family to introduce them to the relatives and friends still living in Saskatchewan and Manitoba. Luella also accompanied the family to help mother with the "little" boys as they were commonly referred to. I, John, Lydia, Peter and Elfrieda were left to hold the fort for a month. That meant we had to take care of the farm, particularly all the poultry, the livestock and the garden. We managed quite well and enjoyed our responsibility and independence. My reward as chief administrator was to get my first oil painting set. So for a while at least, my newest ambition was to be an artist. I worked diligently at painting Mt Baker, white birches and some still life, but had no instruction. My interest in singing continued and I began singing lessons with Mrs. Logan, a local voice teacher. All of these interests were extremely useful for my elementary teaching career.

Our social life was nurtured and circumscribed in our particular farm setting. After school we were expected to do chores such as gathering eggs, cleaning, grading and packing them into crates for shipment. This was done by the girls in the family together with help from the younger boys. The girls also packed eggs into the hatchery trays and assisted in cleaning the trays after the baby chicks hatched. The older boys had to do the more physical tasks of feeding the chickens, cleaning the barns and milking cows. There were also bigger jobs of spreading manure onto the pasture and hay fields for the boys. The girls hoed and weeded the strawberry rows in the spring and picked them when ripe. In the fall, the old growth had to be trimmed off and weevil bait put into each plant. The boys became adept at driving the tractor at an early age and this skill allowed them to become car and truck drivers at an early age. My brother Edward, who was a slender but tall twelve year old was sent by my mother to take some food to the Mennonite Educational Institute one day. His head barely reached the level of giving him visibility through the windshield, and his size was enough to arouse the suspicion of an RCMP officer who escorted him home and sternly admonished mother for sending her young son on such an errand.

Winters were often severe in the 1940's. I can remember snow to a height of five or six feet. The roads were completely impassable and yet trucks had to come in to pick up our fresh milk, eggs and to deliver feed for the poultry. All the men living on Clearbrook Road cleared the road, digging with shovels, as there were no snowplows. We often had a silver thaw, ice that downed the power lines. That meant disaster for our hatchery. We would have to pack the eggs from the incubators into crates, wrap them with blankets, put them in a warm vehicle and take them across the border to a hatchery in the US that had power.

It was equally disastrous for our laying hens. Father had installed automatic watering stations in the barns. If the temperature was below freezing, the pipes broke or at least prevented water from flowing through. If a hen does not drink for even one day, it will stop laying eggs for a while.

Farming was a very big risk as many things can go wrong. One of the diseases that devastated the flock from time to time was the Newcastle disease that originated in England. This would lay waste to our production, require cleaning of the barns, disinfecting them and starting over with the baby chicks. To add insult to injury, we finally had to get guard dogs to keep thieves at bay, who came during the night and stole chickens for the Vancouver market. Our Doberman pincher was an alert and reliable guard dog with a classic look, but not the family pet. Sandy, the cocker spaniel won our hearts with his mournful eyes. Cats were abundant on the farm, but were never house cats and we did not become personal with them.

The war years were a boon for our poultry farm. Eggs and chickens were in great demand and our farm did extremely well during that period. The increased income allowed us to build a new family home. Our family had nine children by 1944; and the last child, Gerald was born in 1948. Our original cottage had a lean-to added providing two extra bedrooms, but we were still crowded and the cottage construction was not substantial.

Our new house had five bedrooms upstairs and one on the main floor for our parents. It had a living room, a dining room, a large kitchen, a pantry, a laundry room and one bathroom. As well, it had a full basement. It was an amazing achievement for our family. Father asked Luella and me whether we preferred a sloping roof, which meant that our bedroom ceilings would be sloping, and we vigorously argued for that kind of a roof instead of a more boxy structure that would give us better bedroom space. We certainly regretted our choice later and wondered how our father allowed us to sway his preference. He was also open to our choice of colors for painting the bedrooms. For my bedroom, after it was mine alone when Luella began her teaching career, I chose a green color that I had seen at the Chapman's house where I did housework once a week. The color choice was not fortunate and so when father asked whether I really liked it, I did not have the courage to say I didn't. I put a brave face on it and said I did.

The finishing materials were not up to snuff on the house because it was built just after the war and the building materials were of poor quality and or not available. My father had to do a lot of scrounging in the Fraser Valley to find the right lumber, shingles and the like. There was no hardwood so our floors were fir. The tile in the kitchen and bathroom were of very poor quality and show cracks before long. But the house was elegant, new and roomy and our loved family home until our parents retired.

The house was demolished when our family farm was expropriated in the late sixties and the Mouat School was built on the eastern end and a Middle School on the western portion. We took our mother to see it just when it was being demolished. Her philosophical comment was " Es ist alles vergaenglich" (Nothing is permanent).

Our social life was nourished in the church community. Choir practice, which included most of the young people, was such an event. Luella, John and I were permitted to furnish our basement, put up curtains and invite young people for house parties, usually on Sunday afternoons. We played the usual parlour games, sang and enjoyed food that we had prepared for the event. One of my fondest memories is that of caroling as a group on Christmas Eve. We were mostly fortunate during those years to have snow on Christmas Eve and nothing matches Christmas Eve out in the snow with your friends singing till midnight! Mill Lake was the favorite frozen lake for ice skating events that happened at least once or twice a winter. Skates were begged for or borrowed unless one was fortunate enough to own a pair. Huge bonfires were built and many in the community came out to enjoy the rare seasonal recreation. An occasional wiener roast in the park on a summer night was special.

My parents managed to create an environment of family solidarity and strength. We were generally a family of academic achievement and modest economic success. Father took his poultry and hatchery endeavor to a very professional level attending poultry breeder association meetings and constantly consulting with Dr. Jacob Biely, the expert at the University of BC on poultry issues. He was an avid reader and we had many papers and magazine subscriptions.

Our family had one picnic per summer. This meant a day at Cultus Lake, or Harrison Hot Springs, or Stanley Park or Peace Arch Park. Each has its unique memories. One day our family was put on high alert when we were relaxing at Harrison Hot Springs. Suddenly, Henry had disappeared! We were all running about in a panic mode searching for him when he was discovered in a boat off a dock by the lake. He was just a little guy exploring. He had climbed into the boat and could not be seen from the shore. When we rented a rowboat on either Cultus Lake or on Lost Lagoon in Stanley Park there was always this huge anxiety because no one in our family could swim. Peace Arch was safer, but it sometimes included a visit to the beach in White Rock. I can understand why mother found these excursions exhausting. Sometimes, we had a wiener roast as supper in the pasture on our own farm. We thought that was real cool.

At age sixteen, I experienced the pangs of unrequited love. There was a girl in our church community that summer who had come from Manitoba and brought with her a certain charm that captured the attention of a young man I had a crush on. My father must have noticed this and he invited me to accompany him on a trip up the Fraser Canyon to Cache Creek in August. The purpose of the trip was to purchase boxes of ripe tomatoes for canning. Freezers were not available to us at that time and so our family had its own tin can operation to can tomatoes, peas, beans and then like so that father could eat sufficient vegetables. I found the trip through the canyon fascinating. On our return, a wind and rainstorm caused a major rockslide and we had to stay overnight at Siska Lodge. The uniqueness of the experience was expressed in a poem that I wrote and provided a sort of catharsis for my romantic pangs.

WIND AND RAIN

The wind and rain are young and free
Wild as horses upon the range
They dash and swirl.
Then for a moment breathless stand.
With slashing hoof and streaming mane
With thunderous hooves like pellets flying
The wind and rain
Have raced upon the earth's wet face.

They paused upon the mountainside
They sniffed and pawed the ground
Hurled the rocks to the ground below
Snapped the great trees swaying trunk
Then whipped the black waves to hissing foam
Far, in the canyon below.
All night long their fury wrought
Till dawn broke and found they had left
For another grazing ground.

In 1951, just before leaving home, I experienced regret at having to leave my family and wrote another poem,

FOREBODING

How silent is the evening sky
Its beauteous clouds
Of ever changing splendour
A scene today
Tomorrow yet another
Outlines yon group of trees upon the hill
While shadowy tinges ever new
Complete the quiet harmony.
How troubled is my soul at times

By nameless fears
By dread and ceaseless worry
A turmoil, wild
That will not heed
Nor comfort find in peaceful scenes
It seeks to find a guiding hand
To lead me through life's challenges

Leaving home is not easy. Home lingers forever in the recesses of ones' mind. The details of my early environment and the family of childhood live within me with a primacy that is a form of love. If fed me language, perceptions, sounds, attitudes and prejudices. Nothing has the absoluteness or intensity as the landscapes that I experienced as a child and which I experienced wholly, without reservation.

The family lined up for the family photo on the occasion of our parents 25th Wedding Anniversary in 1952.

My first formal photo was taken in 1951.

The City

Vancouver was a vaguely unattractive city in 1951, and not yet the city it has become. There was an air of prosperity and excitement in the city now that World War II was over. Huge numbers of young men had come to study at the University of British Columbia after the war ended, housing was needed and builders were rushing to fill the gap. The overseas experience of the soldiers and the influx of European displaced persons following the war changed the dynamics of the city and the Fraser Valley. Many erstwhile farmers in the Fraser Valley gave up unreliable incomes derived from farming, settled in Vancouver and took employment where they could find it. This was true of the Mennonites in the Fraser Valley as well. Previously, generally only single young women sought employment as housekeepers in the wealthier homes in Vancouver. For years, these girls had borne the brunt of the cultural transition as well as providing for much needed cash incomes for their parents. Now young as well as older Mennonite families moved to Vancouver. Churches were built and informal communities of Mennonites arose near Main Street and near Fraser Street.

Disappointment rather than excitement colored my response to the city. I had dearly hoped to attend the University of British Columbia, but here I was with second best, teacher training at the Provincial Normal School located at the corner of Twelfth and Cambie, across from City Hall. A friend, Erna Mueller and I found a room on Fourteenth Avenue nearby. We paid the sum of four dollars each a week each. Normal School was not an academic challenge but had its own culture in which our minds were directed to the task of instructing children and the challenge of managing children and a classroom. A good deal of emphasis was placed on morning performances by the dozen or so classes involving music, drama and art. In our year's major production and performance of *The Wizard of Oz*, I played the part of the Tin Man encased in cardboard wrapped in foil. As no one could tell who I was, I had the liberty to sing in a relaxed fashion even though my suit was very awkward.

Up to that point, dancing had not been permitted in our community. Now it was part of the physical education program. My roommate and I took it seriously and made up for our deficiency in this area by practicing in our upstairs bedroom. This was interrupted when the landlady rushed up saying, "Girls, stop, the living room chandelier is swaying and the ceiling may be in danger of falling". I did get an "A" in dance and it was an achievement for me. My attempt at conducting the class choir was not a positive experience. Miss McManus curtly told me that the choir was singing in spite of my conducting, not because of it. It was humbling to say the least. In January we were required to do a month of practice teaching in a Vancouver School in an assigned classroom. The teacher in charge gradually integrated us into lesson planning and teaching. Visiting Normal School instructors as well as the classroom teacher would critique our teaching. This was repeated in the spring after Easter and in June we were issued a Teaching Certificate.

Living in Vancouver was not an exciting experience when ones finances are challenged. I found a housecleaning job after school on Thursday that provided some income. In addition, I worked all day Saturday at the home of Hubert Chapman who was one of the owners of the Chapman

Clothing store in Vancouver. The income was sufficient to pay my rent, food and travel costs. An occasional trip home on the Stage Bus was a welcome relief from the city. I missed home and even the strong smell of our chicken farm was not altogether offensive when I came home to the farm. Occasionally, a group of my former MEI friends also in Vancouver, studying nursing or working would get together to hitchhike from Vancouver to Clearbrook. There was safety in numbers after all.

Vancouver was still under the curse of frequent and thick fog as a result of the widespread use of sawdust as well as coal as fuel in furnaces that created incredible pollution in the air resulting in the fog. Even the waterfront was not very desirable as real estate because of the incessant blare of the foghorns to guide marine traffic.

I did not particularly enjoy the culture of the Normal School. The downstairs cafeteria was an unpleasant, cigarette smoke filled room, which I rarely visited. I could not understand how rational human beings would choose to smoke. Fortunately, the culture has changed and smoking is now not acceptable.

I managed my finances to obtain a teaching certificate, ending the year with twelve cents in my pocket. I remember going to the corner grocer at Fourteenth Avenue and Cambie Street and spending the twelve cents on bananas. It felt good!

The challenge now was to find employment. I was encouraged to apply for a position in Vancouver by my homeroom instructor, but I did not follow up on her suggestion. I chose rather to apply in Surrey where I could live with my sister who had already taught there for two years.

My first school was the Hjorth Road two-roomed school on Hjorth Road in Surrey. I taught grades one and two. I recall that I was very tense during the first two weeks and felt like I was an over-wound clock. Slowly, I came to the realization that I could in fact teach and do it well. My interest in art and music served me well as a teacher. Teaching reading, which is the major challenge for the primary students was a challenge I enjoyed thoroughly. This school had been in the community a very long time and even had a May Day celebration with parades, May Queen and attendants and a grand picnic after the parade. In retrospect, a small two-room school is a good place to develop skills. I got an excellent evaluation at the end of the term from the superintendent, K.B. Woodward. The school is still in use and celebrated its 100th Anniversary in 2010.

Somehow, I was recruited by the Teacher's Association of Surrey to participate in the production of the light operetta, Erminie. The operetta was performed in each of the five high schools in the district to raise scholarship funds. I sang the lead female role of Erminie. Looking back, I realize how limited I was in stagecraft. It was a great experience, but very demanding in terms of time and energy. Fortunately, Luella and I were living together in a motel unit in Whalley and as she was teaching morning shift, she did all the cooking and shopping. The next year, I moved to Grosvenor Road School and taught on shift as well as there had been a large post-war increase in children and there were not enough school buildings available. Here, I led a group of children in a volunteer choir. We learned all the lovely English songs such as the Ash Grove, etc. Even though I enjoyed teaching very much, I had not forgotten my dream of continuing my education at the University of British Columbia.

Summer school in Victoria was required for two summers following a year at the Normal School before a permanent teaching certificate would be issued. This was a delightful requirement giving us an excuse for a lovely summer vacation. There was a Canadian Pacific Railroad Ferry that left from downtown Vancouver to Victoria. Our Kodak snapshots show us on board wearing hats, gloves and fine dresses and coats. We usually found accommodations in private homes for the six weeks. The classes were not onerous and there was sufficient time for beach parties, swimming lessons at the Empress Hotel pool and sightseeing in and around Victoria. We visited the various churches and received invitations to the church events for young people. This interaction with both the Plymouth Brethren as well as the Baptists was probably my first ecumenical experience and opened my mind to accept the Christian community beyond our Mennonite community.

Romance was very much part of the Victoria experience. Many of us had formed significant attachments during our high school days or later. The Mennonite teachers were scattered across British Columbia from Vancouver to Pouce Coupe. This was an isolated northern community, that had been held up to us during our teacher training as our possible teaching destination. With so many teachers back together during the summer, relationships were either strengthened or severed. I had developed a fondness for a young man who taught in McBride with whom I had been corresponding over two years. The second year in Victoria, I came to the realization that we were not sufficiently well matched. This was not an easy decision as I had made a huge emotional investment, in this, my first serious relationship. To break up the relationship was a devastating experience even though rationally I thought it was the right decision to make. As usual, I composed a poem to reflect my inner turmoil and emotional pain. The poem deals with the contradictory compulsions of the heart as against the restraint of the mind and compares the resulting emotions to the actions of a moth repeatedly flying against a light bulb to its detriment. It took a long time for the heart to mend.

My Grade One class in Grosvenor Road School is sitting for the formal photograph. Teaching was a good experience.

The Campus Encounter

Having cleared that aspect of my life, I was free to pursue my University education in 1954 to 1955. The University of British Columbia is a dominating presence on the western edge of Point Grey. The endowment lands separate the campus from the residential part of Vancouver. It has the benefit of being surrounded on the south, north and west side by the Pacific Ocean and by the forested endowment lands on the east side which have become the Pacific Spirit Park. The University was British Columbia's first and only University until Simon Fraser University was established in 1970.

The university campus in Vancouver was a dream destination for me. The main library with its rows of study tables and easy access to books was of course the central focus of social life. It was the time of co-ed good looks and aspirations to be frosh queen, football queen and sorority pledge. As a Mennonite girl, this was of course out of bounds for me but at least I could be an observer to this exotic milieu of students. The student population was not overwhelmingly large and so a strong sense of community developed through the shared classes and study hall interaction. My connections and friendships came through the Christian Inter Varsity club. It had strong leadership and a variety of stimulating series of speakers as well as social events on campus and in Vancouver homes. Again, my inter-faith experience was broadened and enhanced. There were many other clubs available to students and I enjoyed several of them.

I lived off campus fairly near the University Gates. During my first year, my roommate was Anne Konrad. We had a room in the home of the Parrots just off Trimble and 2nd Avenue. Nearby, Harvey Dyck and several friends lived in rented rooms. Harvey had an old Edsel that was minus its front grill. That left a gaping cavity in the front and we christened the vehicle "the culture vulture". Every morning, until the end of February, Harvey and his friends would roll the vehicle down the hill on Fourth Avenue to start the vehicle, swing it around and come roaring up the hill, fling open the doors while Anne and I jumped in as the vehicle moved slowly and we were off to the university. The car insurance became due on the last day of February and by that time, Harvey could not afford to pay for it, so the car was parked and we hitch hiked or took the bus. Hitch hiking was not an unusual transportation solution in those days, even for young women.

My English 200 instructor was Professor Tor Larsen, an emeritus professor who was an institution at the University. He was a marvelous and inspirational teacher and we hung on his every word. Professor Soward, another UBC institution and his assistant, Professor Norris taught History 101. The class was huge. The teaching was strong. A Fine Arts 200 course taught by Professor McNairn began with primitive and prehistoric art and continued through to the Renaissance. German 200 was an easy course for those of us who had come from the MEI and was enjoyable for its content and no stress quality.

Jean Coulthard Adams, a well-known Vancouver composer taught History of Music 101. She was very knowledgeable and inspirational in introducing me to Renaissance to Modern Theory of Composition and required us to compose a piece as our final submission. Since I was a singer, not an instrumentalist, I composed a Vocalise. In my spare time, as a member of the Mussoc Society, I was part of the Oklahoma production.

The course that had the greatest impact on me was Sociology 200 taught by Kaspar Naegele. As our major assignment he required us to see three movies and analyze their sociological content. The class had to do this assignment with a partner and Gerda Van Dyck and I spent countless hours on this task. Up to that point in my life, I had not seen any movies. Now we were required to see each of the movies three times, record the type of audience present and the emotional reactions of the audience to the movies. Each of the movies was then analyzed as representative or misrepresentative of American Society. Each of the movies was analyzed in respect to background and plot; themes such as honesty, love, sacrifice, and violence; symbolism; roles of characters and institutions; and finally our interpretations of audience reactions. A further requirement was to obtain the original scripts from the producers and then reflect on the producer's conceptions and audience demands. Lastly, we were to draw inferences from the value patterns of American Society.

Professor Naegele was a brilliant professor who had escaped the holocaust but he suffered depression as a result of his experiences in Nazi Germany and eventually committed suicide. I found a personal interview with him very engaging in that he asked me how I could be such an optimistic person. I had not realized to that point that I was by nature very optimistic about life and rarely suffered depressive times. The movies, Gerda and I chose for this assignment were "Carmen Jones", "A Star is Born" and "On the Waterfront". A further requirement was some physical education course. I took, what I considered an exotic option, namely, golf. I never actually set foot on a golf course for at least 30 years after this introduction.

I taught school during May and June of the same year. As I had depleted my finances, I had to teach two more years in order to go back to UBC to finish my Arts degree. I went back to Surrey where I always was welcome and taught at K.B. Woodward School. This time I taught Grade Three and music in the intermediate grades.

Getting back to the world of work after intensive study was a comfortable way to assimilate the education I had received. It also provided me with the opportunity to sing in choirs such as the Fraser Valley Choir conducted by Menno Neufeld for many years. We sang many of the great oratorios such as Handel's Messiah, Mendelssohn's Elijah, and Hayden's Creation. I also continued my voice training with Vancouver teachers such as Anna Nichols. Anna Nicholls had come to Vancouver from China. She was a White Russian who had fled to China after the Russian Revolution. Unfortunately she had become addicted to opium in China and even though her students knew this and the law enforcement officers in Vancouver knew this, she was able to live her life in a small apartment on Seymour Street in downtown Vancouver without harassment. She was an excellent teacher who had received classical Russian training.

I took two major courses at the University during the summer of 1956. One course was American History with a visiting U.S. professor. I recall that one weekend he took a trip on B.C. Rail from Vancouver to Prince George and back. He was appalled at the logging practices in B.C. forests. He spent the better part of an hour in class railing at the lack of government supervision and control. The History as well as the English Course was fascinating in that so much of the religious history such as revival movements and leading religious figures featured prominently in the history of the U.S. In addition, I took a course on American Literature that balanced the History very well. As my early education was oriented toward English History, it was a good thing to become acquainted with our neighbor to the south, especially as the influence of the U.S. on Canada in every possible way has been profound. The American Literature, too, has been profoundly influenced by its religious heritage.

I had some romantic involvements during this period of time but nothing that satisfied me. It seems I had become very critical and developed some fundamental requirements to be met before I would engage in a serious relationship. I had many phone calls, letters and approaches by interested young men, but did not respond to them. Not that I wasn't searching for the "right" person, but I was very careful not to commit my heart before I was sure my head was in agreement.

During the summer of 1957, I took two courses at UBC. Helmut Blume, a German pianist then living in Montreal, taught a course on Music Appreciation. Not only was he very knowledgeable, but also he made the class very interesting by giving us performances of almost all the music he discussed. He was particularly fond of Mozart and gave us a great summer of Mozart performances. The other course was a very pedantic education course in professional training called "Problems in Intermediate teaching". It was probably the most boring course I have ever been subjected to. The instructor organized his information under headings that usually had a dozen or more subheadings. Somehow, information, not balanced by insights is deadly.

In the fall of 1957, I returned to UBC and enrolled in a heavy course load in order to graduate in the spring of 1958. English was my major and to round out my education, I took Shakespeare (413) with Professor Akrigg and Contemporary Literature (434) with Professor Lewis. My other major was History. Father Hanrahan taught Medieval History (304) and Classical Studies (331) with the well-regarded and flamboyant Malcolm McGregor. The Classical Studies has been invaluable in understanding Greek and Roman history. One final education course in Educational Philosophy (400) taught by Professor Argue rounded out my undergraduate degree.

Father Hanrahan was our Medieval History instructor. I regret being ignorant of our ethnic and family connection to the activity of the Hanseatic League during the Medieval period and as a result I missed an opportunity to engage in some fruitful research. Only much later, when my brother Henry saw a painting of the Family Hermann Sudermann in the Art Gallery in Fort Worth, Texas, did we discover the pivotal role played by Heinrich Sudermann in the activities of the Hanseatic Trade League. My brother Henry was able to do some further research when he was a banker in London, England. He discovered that Heinrich Sudermann had an office in the 1500's in London just a few blocks from where Henry now worked for the Bank of British Columbia. Heinrich Sudermann, son of Hermann Sudermann, was trained as a lawyer and banker and was the head of the Hanseatic Trading League for many years. Later, during our travels, we found streets in Cologne, Antwerp and Bruge named after this family. We have done considerable research, but have not found the connecting links with this medieval family, particularly after the move of members from the Netherlands to Poland. My father said that family stories passed down say that the Sudermans came out of the village of Dortmund, which is where this illustrious family came from. Another interesting aside is that in his letters, Erasmus, the great humanist states that he stayed in the home of the Sudermans when he traveled by horseback from Basil back to the Netherlands.

One of the poets we studied in Professor Lewis's class was Gerard Manley Hopkins. I very much resonated with his poetry and wrote my term paper on Hopkins. The professor submitted the essay in the competition for the fourth year Book Prize. It was chosen as the best essay in the graduating year and I was pleased with the honour acknowledged during my graduation.

I enjoyed the summer of 1958, at summer school again! I indulged my artistic instincts and signed up for an intensive Art Course with Sam Black. We spent four hours every day sketching, painting, exploring techniques such as silk screen, design with fabrics, etc. It was a wonderfully relaxing and creative summer.

I have since painted from time to time, however, there have been so many priorities that have developed in the midst of life that I have more or less shelved painting for a while. I am thinking of picking it up when I no longer golf, travel as much and have less mobility.

The most significant event of the summer was in meeting with John Friesen who was also a summer school student. He managed to anticipate my routine and we had some pleasant conversations on a daily basis. But, he never asked me for a date. That fall he was a teacher at the private Mennonite School in Yarrow. I was now teaching at Templeton High School in Vancouver. I was annoyed at his failure to ask me for a date and so I ignored him completely at the fall Teacher's Conference which we both attended. That was the beginning of our romance.

Templeton is in east Vancouver and was a challenging teaching experience for me. The population has a strong ethnic mix with a predominance of the Italian sector. The size of the students in the hallways was intimidating as I was only 26 years old at the time and felt not much older than the students. The most dreaded task was to supervise the flow of students as they walked continuously round and round the hallways on rainy days when they could not go outside during recess and the lunch break. I was overwhelmed by the boisterous culture of youth. I did not think I would stay in High School teaching but by the second year, I had established a good reputation, had the respect and affection of the students and began to enjoy the challenges.

I did not have training in Guidance and Counseling subjects, but in the second year I was asked to take on the role of girl's counselor as well as teaching English. My favorite subject to teach was always English. Students at Templeton were grouped in classes according to ability. Teachers were given some good, some average and some not so good classes. As counselor, I had the dubious pleasure of getting the class with the lowest achievement in their English class. At the end of the year, the scores of these girls ranked average. This I considered a great success. From this class also, a girl who had failed twice in her grades during her lifetime won the public speaking contest for her grade. That was a huge victory and morale booster for the girls in this class. I found that, even the most rambunctious class of boys, could be mesmerized by an oral reading of Treasure Island or A Christmas Carol.

I have found that teaching English gives one enormous opportunity to influence the thinking of students. To me, literature is full of psychological insights, moral values, religious thought and human wisdom. It speaks in the language of ordinary people and not in rhetoric peculiar to a particular discipline. It allows discussion and reflection on issues relevant to young people even more than a guidance class provides. It allows for value judgment and inspiration at the same time.

At home, in the Fraser Valley, on the poultry farm, father was introducing new breeding stock and gaining an excellent reputation. He had brought the new strain of Demler White Leghorns from a breeder in Anaheim, California to B.C. He was selling the baby chicks to Fraser Valley farmers. He entered his hens in the egg-laying contest at the Pacific National Exhibition in August of 1958 and won over 28 other entries. He had the ability to choose good laying hens and his hens laid 62 out of a possible 70 eggs. There was a picture of him in the local newspaper, the Abbotsford, Sumas and Matsqui News with his trophies as well as a picture of his expanded hatchery following his triumph. We teased father a good deal about his picture taken with Miss PNE that was printed in the Vancouver Sun and a framed copy hung in his bedroom. He continued to offer the traditional New Hampshire chicks and the Grey Leghorn Cross chicks as well. The advantages of the Demler White Leghorn was that " it stands confinement well, has high resistance to Leukosis, lays heavily over a long period of time and has excellent egg quality along with good egg size". By this time hens were no longer on a free range or even confined to a barn but were kept in stacked cages. He won at the Exhibition for almost as long as he made entries. When the chickens hatch, they have to be distinguished as to sex as some farmers wish to raise cockerels for slaughter and others want only pullets for egg laying purposes. It was a usual request that father would make – phone the sexers to come, the chicks have hatched. The local sexers would arrive and diligently peer at the poor chick's posterior to determine their sex. The sexers had a high ratio of success on that score.

Our parents met the challenges of a dispersing family. Our home was always a demanding economic unit. Having animals is like tending young children. Morning noon and night they must be fed and cared for. Neglect brings economic ruin. Our parents had the constant chore of keeping the children motivated in performance of the daily chores. It is particularly difficult to constantly adjust to the changing status of family members.

As the family members grew up, they left home to study or enter their professions. Luella taught four years, and then married Henry Unger in 1953. Since Henry was a teacher at the MEI, the wedding was huge and held in the MEI auditorium. Weddings in those days involved all church members, relatives and acquaintances. Church basement receptions were held in shifts and young people and others served the food, washed the dishes and cleaned up after the reception. Luella and Henry bought their first little home on Mt Lehman Road.

Brother John had taken teacher training in 1952 after spending a year at the Mennonite Brethren Bible College in Winnipeg and was teaching in the Fraser Valley. He was married to Susan Enns, my friend, in 1957. Their first home was just off Clearbrook Road. Then they moved to Prince George where he taught and was a principal for the rest of his career.

Lydia entered nurses training in 1954. She was the family dynamo, full of entertaining stories of her life in Vancouver. She would bring numerous classmates home for weekend visits and always leave mother with reassuring promises about her activities. In retrospect, I don't know how our parents dealt with all the demands of their children and yet maintained their equilibrium

Peter came to UBC in 1956 to earn a Commerce Degree. In the year 1957 to 1958, Peter, Elfrieda and I lived together in Vancouver. Peter had an old black vehicle, which gave us mobility. I finally got sufficient courage to learn to drive it. Up to that point, I had not driven a car. I had father coach me before I took my driver's license. I failed! I had never failed anything before. What an embarrassment! The skill of backing into a parallel parking space was what tripped me up. Father had forgotten about that one. So I learned that skill and got my driver's license. Peter and Erica Sawatsky got married in 1962.

Elfrieda came to UBC in 1957 to take her teacher training. She had been dating Ernie Block for some time. He was attending the Mennonite Brethren Bible College in Winnipeg. He also obtained his teaching degree and both of them taught in northern BC. Prince George became their long time home.

Not one of the sons would offer to take over the farm. Jack, Henry and Edward were making their mark as athletes. The MEI basketball team was beginning to make headlines during the March tournaments. In the early sixties, Ed achieved "Most Valuable Player' status on the provincial level for several years. The MEI team also won the provincial cup in 1963. In due course, they all left the family farm and found their way to UBC.

Jack went to Toronto as well as Anaheim to gain knowledge on the poultry business. He did not stay on the farm. He took an Arts Degree and initially entering teaching. He moved on to various other business ventures and settled into financial planning.

Henry came to UBC and obtained a degree in Chemical Engineering. He worked for Monsanto in the US until he was about to be drafted into the US army to go to Vietnam. He then got an MBA and went into banking. He was transferred to Dallas, Texas where he met and married Rhonda.

Ed continued his superb career as an athlete at Seattle Pacific University. Eventually he left his basketball career to finish his studies at UBC. He entered law and married his childhood sweetheart, Ingrid Sawatsky.

Gerald found his passion at the Abbotsford Airport and became an avid flyer. He was soon taking family members on flights, dropping skydivers and generally enjoying his new freedom in the sky.

In 1959, I bought a car. What luxury! I remember a schoolteacher at Templeton, who was on exchange from England, chastising me for such a ridiculous purchase. Very few people, especially single people had vehicles in England she said. It was also a serious environmental issue that I should be aware of was her further concern. She certainly was ahead of her time on that issue.

In the same year, John Friesen asked me out on a date. Since he had not too recently broken his engagement and ended his relationship with another young woman, I was somewhat hesitant about the propriety of accepting this invitation. However, I felt that he was a very sensitive and competent young man, so I decided to take the risk. Our relationship proceeded very quickly and we were married on April 18, 1960. I was living in an apartment on Cambie Street. John lived at his mother's house at 44th Avenue and Main Street. I believe we spent nearly every evening together from November until we were married on April 18th, 1960. Our favourite haunt was Little Mountain and that park has some excellent memories for us. He probably won my heart as well as my mind by his willingness to have deep and meaningful discussions with me. He was not yet a psychologist, but had the gift of listening and drawing me out to share my innermost thoughts. In many ways, I had learned not to make myself vulnerable to people and it was a great pleasure to share with this kindred spirit. Our life together has been enormously enriching for us both.

After various engagement parties with our families, showers and teas, the Easter Monday wedding day arrived very quickly. Again, we had one of these very large Mennonite weddings. It was held in the Clearbrook Mennonite Brethren church, which was my home church. Since we had both been attending Fraserview Mennonite Brethren Church in Vancouver, and both of us invited friends and teaching colleagues, the numbers were large. Our honeymoon was in Harrison Hot Springs as we only had the week after Easter as a holiday before we had to be back at school. Life after that accelerated and we have never looked back. I did not write any poetry for a very long time.

Our wedding photo, taken April 18th, 1960.

Marriage

John and I were ready for the adventure of marriage. We were both twenty-eight and had had sufficient time to discover who we were and what our life's aspirations were. In spite of the fact that our previous romantic ventures had failed, we were optimistic about the potential of our relationship. There were strengths that John had that I did not have. He was sensitive and understanding. He was always ready to engage in opportunities and not daunted by difficulties. He was a visionary in many ways. He had a ready smile and easy approach toward people. I was more reserved. I could be relied on to pick up the challenge and carry through a project he lost interest in. I had the determination, which gave me the resources to implement his visions. Visions are essential, but fail unless there is the ability to actualize them. Perhaps my greatest contribution is the ability to be the competent "helpmeet" a woman is destined to be. In spite of this fact in the era of women's liberation, I too found my own path of liberation. I have always taken the position that I have to do what I am uniquely called to do, to respond to my inner direction.

To marry someone is to invite the opportunity to change from what you are into a new form and entity. The symbolic blowing out of your individual candle and lighting the unity candle is not something we did during our marriage ceremony. But in hindsight, I did blow out the candle of my former life and light a new candle of existence, which in many ways was quite different from my life before marriage. Living with a person who adds his aspirations and experience to yours in the making of decisions on a day-to-day basis changes what you think and do. For example, the culture of my family was basically very similar in some ways but radically different than the culture of John's family in other ways. His family was very oriented towards business undertakings, interested in investing in real estate and in participating in economic ventures. My family had no such interest or experience. His family had a history of taking risks. My family was risk adverse. His family was inclined to think in visionary ways; my family thought in practical and modest terms about the world and opportunities.

Our agenda for living also changed because of new necessities and interests. The first experience I had of this change in how things are done was the purchase of our first house. We lived in a rented apartment for only six months and very quickly bought a house on Crown Street in Vancouver. The house was bought separately from the city and moved onto a lot purchased from the city. The city was in the process of building a sewage plant on Iona Island and the main outfall pipe went down Olympic Street where this house had been built. The City expropriated the property and we purchased the house from the City. John's brother Pete had a house moving business and moved the house for us. Of course, John's knowledge of such a possibility gave us that particular opportunity. My family would never have checked the newspaper for such opportunities nor would it have had any idea of the financial gain that could be achieved.

The move of the house to the new lot was made overnight but there were several months of hard work in putting the house back together. This undertaking of renovation and restoration was another new experience for me and a harbinger of many more undertakings related to real estate to come in my life. Our home was on Crown Street at the edge of beautiful Musqueam Park, which forms a green belt between the city of Vancouver and the Musqueam Indian Reserve.

The overlapping of goals was another significant change for me. To obtain my university degree, I had slowly but surely earned my way through teaching and then taking time off for studies. Even on the day of the Friesen family's celebration of our engagement at John's home, he disappeared into his bedroom to study for his Master's exams that fell the next day. I had never operated on such a tight schedule.

By December of our first year, he proposed that we take a chance on getting pregnant; I did get pregnant at once. This was a risk that we took, even though we were aware of the existing School Board policy that women who were pregnant were not allowed to teach. I managed to complete the teaching year to the end of June because I am fairly tall and even though Ingrid was born on August 26th. I was not showing very much under my shirtwaist dress by the end of June.

John and I had a common Mennonite heritage and a very similar community experience. My experience had been in Abbotsford, while his was in Yarrow. Both of our church tradition was Mennonite Brethren. He had attended the Sharon High School; I had attended the Mennonite Educational Institute. We now were part of the group that left the Fraserview Mennonite Brethren Church to become part of the new Killarney Park Mennonite Brethren Church in Vancouver. This church was built to serve the rapidly growing Mennonite population in Vancouver. John was a Sunday school teacher and Youth leader, we both sang in the choir and I soon joined the ranks of mothers in the baby room with my new baby.

Before marriage, I had had a considerable time of independence and professional experience. It was a drastic change for me to stay at home when September came. Even though Ingrid was a beautiful baby, I had a lovely home and no worries, I remember being vaguely unhappy. I went for walks and enjoyed my neighborhood, but I was lonely and missed the daily connections work gives you. I missed the adventure and challenges out there. Since I was the second of ten children, I did not find mothering an overwhelming challenge. In one of the MEI yearbooks, the caption below my picture was “efficiency is her name”. I was an efficient person and so I had time on my hands. I had no connections in the neighborhood except for one somewhat older neighbor, Marge Murray. We picked blackberries together on what was the Musqueam Reserve, made blackberry jam, consulted on our gardens and landscaping, but I was still alone a good deal of the time. Marge Murray was part of the well-known Murray Nursery family that had lived in the Kerrisdale area.

The radio was my only connection to the world out there. Even at that there were no talk shows on the radio and we had no television set until we moved to Edmonton. The hours dragged on before John would arrive home from his teaching at Winston Churchill High School. Two of my brothers, Jack and Henry came to live with us in September of 1961. They were students at the University. That gave me more to do as we provided room and board for them.

Ingrid Anne Friesen, born August 26th, 1961
in Vancouver, British Columbia

Edmonton

John had said before we were married, that he wished to get his doctorate as a psychologist and I had thought that was a good idea. So the next major undertaking was to sell our home and move to Edmonton. To our great surprise, when we left in August for Edmonton, I was several months pregnant with our second child. I nursed Ingrid and all of the children and so I was not sure when Carolyn had been conceived. In fact our first two children were seventeen months apart, our second and third child were seventeen months apart and our third and fourth child were twenty-nine months apart. We had obviously hesitated somewhat at the fourth project. I never really had time to think about how things would be from then on, they just happened. After renting for two years, the urge to buy got the uppermost and we bought a house in Edmonton. We bought a relatively modest new house in Lendrum Place, quite near the Lendrum Mennonite Brethren Church, which was newly established in that area.

We were in for some major adjustments in Edmonton. We found the Alberta landscape to be cold and sterile in comparison to British Columbia. John's doctoral studies were extremely demanding with a great deal of weekly reading required. I had a year old infant, was pregnant and had limited social connections as well as limited income. Carolyn was born on January 25th when Edmonton was at its coldest. I was in the Royal Alexandra Hospital in Edmonton. To keep the cold out, the nurses put towels on the window sills. There were four women to a room and the most objectionable experience was to share a room with two women who smoked non-stop! It was amazing that the hospital in those days permitted smoking on the wards and even with infants in the room. The final insult was that one of the women was afraid of the dark and kept her light on all night. It was an experience from hell. The only way I kept my sanity was to read. I read the book, "Cheaper by the dozen" and enjoyed it thoroughly, sometimes wondering if that might be a possible future for me.

The situation at home proved to be another challenge. We had hired a Mrs. Thiessen to look after baby Ingrid while John went to his classes. Unfortunately, her daughter who drove her to our house was involved in an accident during her first day driving her mother to our house, and so John lent her our car. This meant he came to visit me once during the eight-day hospital stay. All in all, it would have been better for me to go home after one day as the women do today to avoid the nightmare of my hospital experience and to be there for Ingrid. The worst was yet to come. When I got home, Ingrid was throwing up and had diarrhea because she had been fed baby food that had gone bad. She was so weak she could hardly walk. Carolyn immediately developed an allergy to scented baby powder and her face and eyes became red and swollen. John succumbed to the general pressure of studies and home. His back seized up and he was immobilized in bed for three days. It was tough. After a week, everyone recovered and life went on.

Life for women with husbands who are studying has always been difficult. In retrospect I am aware that this situation was common among women. Many worked if they were not pregnant and earned enough income to support their husbands throughout the period of their husband's education. I remember many afternoon walks in the Strathcona neighborhood along the ridge that bordered the Saskatchewan River. I sewed my own clothes and little items for Ingrid as well as for the new baby. It seemed my shopping habits of buying good quality clothes changed. The Army and Navy store became a place where I found good bargains.

In Edmonton I discovered the Holt Renfrew store that had not as yet come to Vancouver at that time. I bought a fancy black velvet hat with a floppy brim that I thought to be very elegant. I wore it when we traveled to Vancouver over the Christmas holidays with my three quarter length muskrat fur coat. As we were waiting for the shuttle for the airport, at the Hotel McDonald, an inebriated, but well-dressed man approached me and said, "Lady, you are very good looking, but that hat looks awful". I felt deflated, but wore the hat nonetheless and received many compliments for it.

It was always a physical shock to return to Vancouver over the Christmas break. The dry, crisp and very cold Edmonton weather was what we experienced as we boarded the plane on the tarmac and the moist warm feeling of a bathroom greeted us as we stepped off the plane in Vancouver. In those days, boarding and deplaning was not done under covered walkways. Every year of the four years that we lived in Edmonton, we spent some time in British Columbia over the summer. It has to be said that almost every time we made the big expedition, one or more of the children would come down with the mumps, the measles or just colds. It would take me at least two weeks to recover a comfortable schedule with the children upon our return to Edmonton. It also took me at least a several weeks to gain my strength back.

After we moved into our home in Lendrum, I felt much more settled. We lived a half a block away from the church and it was easier to manage the infants to and from visits to the church. If any of them proved too much on a Sunday morning, I could simply take them home and put them to bed. Also, it took only minutes to go to and from the church so that attendance and regular participation was much easier than if one has to commute for thirty minutes or more.

During March the outdoors in Edmonton looked very grungy. The snow had become gray from all the sanding. There was very little growth that showed any greenery. I would clip dead branches from bushes and put them in water to enjoy their sprouts after a few weeks. Somehow, it takes a while to open one's eyes to beauty that is inherent in every landscape. I finally appreciated the big blue skies in Edmonton that I had loved as a child in Manitoba. I began to see the glorious sunsets that outlined the quiet farmlands and fields. I respected the unbelievable cold of minus thirty or more and the chill it gave to the perimeter of the rooms even though the furnace was hard at work. Cold penetrated the house to such a degree, that the lumber in the walls contracted with ominous crackling.

Fashions for women dictated long coats and high boots during the early sixties. It was the perfect choice for Edmonton winter weather. One could stand at a bus stop without freezing to death, snug in a long coat and boots. Stomping around in an overheated store was another matter.

Many of the families living in our neighborhood, had young children and so there was opportunity to make play dates in the morning. Every afternoon, after naptime all the mothers would bundle up their children in winter time and come out for a sleigh ride and a visit with the other moms. Of course, by the time the third child was snugly bundled up in snowsuit, boots, mittens and hat, the first child would have to be unbundled for a trip to the bathroom.

We got a black and white television set shortly before John Kennedy was assassinated and began to see the world events in our home. Television provided entertainment for the house bound winter periods for us as well as the children. Summertime was much enjoyed and the months of May, June, July and August are excellent in Edmonton. After work, we would hurry down to the parks in the river valley, barbecue our supper and play with the children until bedtime. Our gardens, which lagged far behind the BC gardens, took off and we often had ripe tomatoes before my mother had them in her BC garden. The long hours of daylight were a distinct advantage to us all, plants and humans.

Friends became the most important part of the life we lived in Edmonton. The significance of friends in the life of young adults was experienced most dramatically when we were removed from our family connections as well as from the friendships we had made as we grew up in the Fraser Valley. We found our community of friends very stimulating. Among our Mennonite connections, many were young families who had come to Edmonton from southern Alberta to either study or find employment. With no extended family to spend time with we had more time to relate to friends. Conversations were often deep and engaging. Social events were hilarious. Dr. Peter Bargen and his wife, Anne were gracious hosts to the younger couples. Peter Rempel was the pastor of the new church group and he and his wife Mary were engaging and lively. Werner and Teena Schmidt, John and Lenora Pauls, Jake and Irene Isaak, Helga and George

Loewen, Tena and Rudy Wiebe and so many others entered into a robust and productive life in the academic, professional and economic opportunities that were plentiful in Edmonton. We were exhilarated and stimulated to engage in the opportunities that presented themselves.

After one year at the university, John completed his course requirements for a Doctorate in Psychology. He then undertook the research for his thesis and wrote the thesis over the next three years. As usual, he also looked for employment. He was hired by the Province of Alberta's Department of Education as Head of Counseling Services for the province. It was quite a heady experience. He was only thirty-two years of age. In a province where Premier Ernest Manning had taken on the job of premier at the age of twenty-six years, this was not unusual. In Vancouver as well as British Columbia generally, only very senior people got the important jobs.

This job gave him many opportunities for professional growth. He was asked to give the keynote address at many conferences as well as to professional educators around the province. He traveled the length and breadth of Alberta for the purpose of school inspections. Summer and winter, he would be away from home at least one week every month.

One of the benefits of this job was that he was expected to attend conferences such as those sponsored by the American Psychological Association that were held every year in cities across the U.S. This became an opportunity for me to take much needed vacation time with John. We went to cities such as Minneapolis, San Francisco and Washington. D.C. I would arrange care giving for our young family for the four or five days with trusted friends. The APA conferences were huge, usually spread over five or six hotels with about eleven hundred attendees. There were interesting events organized for spouses during the day such as city tours and entertainment. I would attend keynote speakers such as major author's presentations over lunch or dinner with John. As we were always in big cities, shopping opportunities were a desirable option during the day and a morning in bed was a luxury not to be missed. Travel connected with conferences became a way of life for us, starting in Alberta.

The relatively small church group met in a school building for a few years and then undertook the building of the education wing in Lendrum Place. This church experience was a much more intimate and meaningful experience than the big churches we had participated in Vancouver. Since that experience, I have much preferred a small house church experience to a large congregation.

Participation is the factor of real worship, not just attendance. When a church becomes large, the leadership is in control not the worshippers. As Anabaptists, lay leadership has always been a strong component until the dynamics of large communities change this approach. Unfortunately, the Mennonite Brethren Churches constantly adopt the traditions of other denominations, installing multiple pastors and creating a top down model of church structure. This results in the move away from participation according to giftedness to rigid rejection of participation by women in worship and administration and a centralization of power in a male eldership model common in many churches today. In many ways, the mega church model has hijacked the church experience from its members.

Even though my life was governed by pregnancy and the demands of infant children during the four years we lived in Edmonton, I sang as often as I could in groups and as a soloist in the church. Music was an every day necessity. We regularly attended the Edmonton Symphony events on Saturday nights.

During our last year in Edmonton, Tom Ralston introduced the Suzuki Method of teaching string instruments to Edmonton residents. The Suzuki method was a very effective method of teaching music based on the principle that every one can learn the language they are exposed to and so every one can learn music if they are properly exposed to music. Our friend, Lenora Pauls was a pianist and her husband, John Pauls a violinist and so it was essential that their four-year old John David would be a candidate for violin lessons. At that time, Lenora had no car at her disposal and I could arrange for John to leave me his on certain days. Since I had four year old Ingrid, two and a half year Carolyn and year old John, I had not even thought of music lessons. However, Lenora volunteered to look after my two while Ingrid and I had lessons if I took on the task of driving us all to lessons. This was the beginning of the strong role of music in our family. Ingrid became proficient and continued to play until she was in Grade Twelve. Carolyn also started and played the violin until she graduated from High School. Together with John, they became members of the Delta Youth Orchestra. Ken too played in the Junior Orchestra. Harry Gomez was the girl's instructor, as well as the youth orchestra conductor. He was a very demanding instructor and in hindsight, not the right taskmaster for the girls. John's first cello instructor was Peggy Gibson, a motherly encouraging teacher. He also benefited greatly from the support and instruction of both Hans Siegrist and Tony Elliot, the concertmaster of the Vancouver Symphony.

Alberta has been the land of opportunity for many people in many sectors of the economy. The other startling realization for us was that this province had the Midas touch of gold, in this case black gold - oil. We noticed that the high schools were well built with wide hallways and indoor swimming pools. There was rarely a provincial debt. Our utilities and other costs were almost one half of what we paid in Vancouver. Housing was relatively cheap as there is almost unlimited availability of land. We began to appreciate the positive aspects of this province.

As Director of Counseling Services, John was invited by many school related organizations to give speeches all over the province. I was recruited as the typist and more, as the assistant speechwriter. I can remember typing in my highly pregnant state leaning backwards to accommodate my large stomach and suffering backache and fatigue in the process. John would travel a great deal, up to a week at a time from Fort Vermillion in the north to Taber in the south and all the in between stops doing inspections and connecting with the various superintendents of schools. On weekends, he was doing his experimental work at the University and collecting his data for his thesis. It was a very busy time for all us. It meant that with the arrival of our third child, I needed help and a young girl was my house help during July and August of 1964. John Howard was born on July 12th of that year.

In 1966, John finished his Thesis and received his Doctorate. He began to send out resumes to all the major Universities and began to receive an equal number of job offers. We lived in a time when young graduates had many job offers and a choice of University positions. Of course, we looked favorably on a return to Vancouver and so when UBC offered John a position, he could not but take it.

I was pregnant and hoped for another boy to balance the family. Now we faced selling our home in Edmonton and finding a home in Vancouver

Four year old Ingrid and I, practicing "Twinkle, Twinkle, little Star."

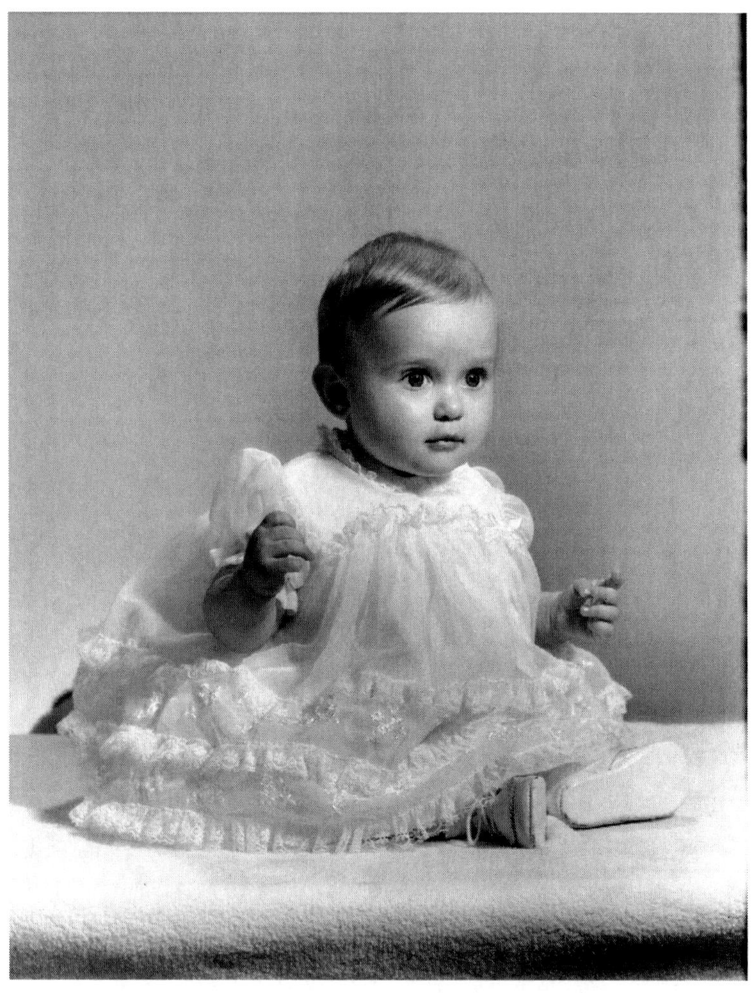

Carolyn Lenore Friesen, born January 25, 1963 in the Royal Alexandra Hospital in Edmonton Alberta.

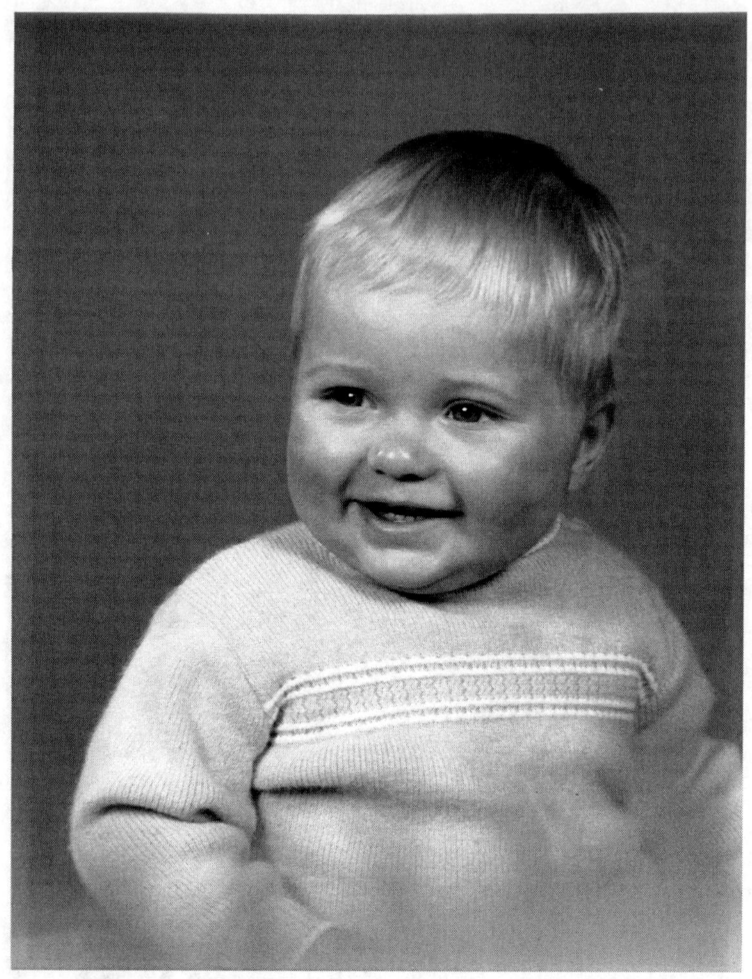

John Howard Friesen, born July 12, 1964 in the Royal Alexandra Hospital in Edmonton, Alberta.

Tsawwassen, by the Sea

In Delta, part of the south western extremity of land partially surrounded by the Pacific ocean lays a high plateau that compromises Tsawwassen, which is part of the municipality of Delta and Point Roberts, which is part of Washington State.

The four years in Edmonton had not been financially helpful. Prices in Vancouver had doubled. The house we sold on Crown Street for $22,000.00 in 1962 was now on the market for $44,000.00. We sold our Edmonton house for $14,000.00. John went to Vancouver by himself in July as I was pregnant and had three little ones under the age of five. He decided that buying a house in Tsawwassen was our best option and purchased a large Tudor style home on a half-acre lot there. It was a lovely home for our family and we lived there for five years until John had so many speeding tickets in his attempts to get to UBC on time, that we decided to move to Vancouver again. During this period of time, the Fraser Street Bridge was shut down and the Arthur Lang Bridge was not yet finished and the only way to get to Vancouver was via the Oak Street Bridge.

During our years in Edmonton, we were preoccupied with our career and our young family. Coming back to Vancouver, we realized that the world was changing. John met this change head on at the University. As a young professor he became aware of the student protest movements. Protest leaders were invading the classes at the university, the faculty club was held hostage for days and a pig was led into the premises. The protestors swilled themselves on the liquor and wine in the faculty club and created chaos on the campus.

These difficult challenges were John's introduction to university teaching. He was also assigned to an evening class and so would go to his mother's home on 44th Street near Main for dinner and not arrive home until late one or two nights a week. Fortunately, we had arranged for an au pair girl through MCC for a six-month period to help us for several months before Ken's birth and for several months after his arrival. Elke was a young girl from Germany who arrived at our home on September first. She proved to be of great help. It was a luxury that I should have continued but did not think necessary as I was so used to managing things myself. Ken came ten days early on December 11th and thoughtfully allowed us to be ready for Christmas.

When we came to Tsawwassen in late August, Ingrid turned five years old and was ready to start Kindergarten. Kindergarten was not yet part of the school system. We enrolled her in St. David's Kindergarten conducted in the Anglican Church. All except Ken attended this Kindergarten. It was very well run and required parent participation one full morning every two weeks. This was the beginning of juggling home duties with school schedules for the next six years until Ken was in Grade One and at school all day together with his siblings. Babysitters, exchanges with other mothers and emergency rearrangements are the constant challenge of mothers scheduling their children's as well as their own lives. Having a car was an essential requirement and for a while, we did not have a second vehicle.

When we sold our house in Vancouver, we had invested some of the profit with one of John's brothers, Jake, who lived in Winnipeg. When we returned to Vancouver, John's brother Pete was engaged in prefabricated housing units for Expo 67 in Montreal. He required funding and offered a high interest rate to us if we would invest with him, which we did. The sad story was that the Quebec construction lobby shut the importing of prefabricated housing down and the Expo management refused to pay for the housing units already on rail flatbeds that had been shipped to Quebec. This forced Pete's company into bankruptcy.

This was the beginning of a sad chapter in Pete's business and family life. Not only had we invested our money with Pete, but also we had persuaded my brother John who had just sold his house in Abbotsford before moving to Prince George, to invest a significant amount with Pete. John and I were both ignorant of proper business practice. We had naively lent money to family members on the basis of trust with no security of any kind. We did not have any notion of proper business practices. John went to see lawyer Bill Mulholland, who lived a few houses up the street from ours in Tsawwassen. He managed to register chattel mortgages against the units sitting in Montreal on CNR flatbeds. John was forced to fly to Montreal, retain a lawyer and with a great deal of effort rescue my brother John's funds as well as ours. This was probably the pivotal personal experience that opened my eyes to the necessity of being somewhat more sophisticated in our financial dealings and led me to enter the practice of law eventually.

It seems that difficult experiences tend to come in threes or more. Another investment we had made before we left Vancouver was to make a gift to the fledgling Trinity

Western University as well as a loan of three thousand to a company called Faith Investments. This company was organized and run by a number of Free Church business men from B.C. and Alberta who sought to make investments in order to support Trinity Western University. John's brother Pete had been instrumental in purchasing the land with the others. He, with his house moving company had moved the first buildings onto the site that were used until more substantial funds were available to build the main structures.

Unfortunately, the company, Faith Investments Ltd, was poorly managed and faced bankruptcy when we returned from Alberta. There was a plan to form a new company that was in fact incorporated. This company was called Malmo Holdings Ltd., the name Malmo taken because it was a favorite Swedish city of some of the shareholders. Many of the Alberta businessmen were in fact of Swedish origin. The intention was to use the company to rescue some of the property facing foreclosure in Faith Investments. At the last minute, the Alberta men backed out, not wishing to throw good money after bad.

We took over the assets and problems of the company. John did all he could to rescue the situation involving property in Powell River and in Squamish, but it was impossible. He spent many hours consulting lawyers, negotiating with contractors, with municipalities trying to gain time to redeem the situation, to delay taxes or to remortgage properties. It was all to no avail. One property remained in Faith Investments. This was the property contiguous to the Trinity property, but across the railroad tracks from it. Since no one wanted to use the company, Malmo Holdings Ltd., we purchased it and then purchased the remaining property from the previous owners. Malmo Holdings has been with us since 1967.

The property in Langley became part of a family adventure. John persuaded our friends, Alice and Alf Siemens to buy a half interest in the property. Our intention had been to divide the property into five-acre plots and sell it. We had just sold two five-acre plots when the New Democratic Party came into power in British Columbia and passed the Agricultural Land Freeze Act. This put an end to any further subdivision as this property was deemed to be agricultural. We then purchased young cattle and raised them for the beef market. This turned out to be an adventure in itself. Cattle often don't respect fences. Our herd managed to stop the trains carrying coal to the port in Point Roberts, to visit cattle next door on Peter Wall's property and to create mayhem whenever possible.

On loading cattle for market, a steer that had not been properly castrated managed to leap over the plywood-loading barrier of the cattle truck and escaped to the neighboring farm. As a last desperate attempt to deal with this ornery creature, my brother Gerald was invited to help with the situation. He arrived with his rifle at five in the morning and brought the beast down just as he rose to his feet. John and Alf had arranged for a local butcher to bring his mobile abattoir to the site. The animal was quickly hung on a tripod and drawn and quartered. Alice claimed that the steak from this animal insisted on jumping out of her fry pan whenever she cooked it!

Tsawwassen is a lovely community to live in, especially if you worked there as well. As a result of the proximity to water and its position in the south of the greater Vancouver area, it was consistently ahead in growth and gardens. We all indulged in the gardening challenges on our half-acre lot. Our back yard was south facing. We built a large patio facing south. John took the Ingrid with him to the shoreline nearby and brought home rocks to build a retaining wall. In addition to a good-sized lawn, we built a fine Japanese garden with a dry streambed crossed by a traditional curved bridge. On the edges of the winding streambed, I planted irises, peonies and other somewhat exotic plants that are favored in such gardens.

John's mother had always had a productive grape vine in her garden. She encouraged us to plant a vine in our patio area. John constructed a fine trellis. The vine grew magnificently. Grape vines require a lot of pruning. The shoots keep coming and if they are not pruned back, the plant will grow wildly and not many grapes will be produced. I learned quickly and was rewarded with seven bundles after one year and seventy in the second year. After that I was dismayed with the abundance of grapes.

Beyond the lawn and Japanese garden lay our garden, a very large garden! We planted fruit trees, raspberries, strawberries and every possible vegetable from asparagus to zucchini. Our cherry tree was astoundingly productive as it was planted right next to the compost box. I found out very soon that gardening was not limited to four months as it had been in Edmonton, but in fact, I was at it from February to November.

Our next-door neighbor, Diane, was an avid member of the Evergreen Garden Club. This club had a long tradition in Delta. Two shows were held, one in spring and one in fall. We became converts and before long our children were competing in the flower and vegetable classes, the dish garden class and any other class that was available to their interests. Diane regularly came home with an armful of trophies as well as a bundle of ribbons.

I was seduced into gardening very gradually. In February, Diane advised me that it was time to plant peas. She was right. They germinated very well in the cool weather. As the season progressed she would provide me with plants from her green house, which I could not resist. She was a very informed gardener. She had every possible seed catalogue and nursery plant magazine and spent a good part of her winter educating herself. She ordered exotic seeds of variations and hybrids of newly developed tomatoes, beans, or whatever intrigued her. I was the beneficiary of her gardening expertise.

The down side of having a lush productive garden is that you have far too many vegetables and fruits to eat so you are forced to give your bounty away. Giving vegetables away in Tsawwassen where everyone has a good garden is not easy!

The isolation of Tsawwassen allows it to become a community where one gets to connect with many neighbours. There was a strong sense of community and strong participation in community activities, including the arts. I began to take up painting with an enthusiastic night class instructor. Across the border, in Point Roberts were many art shops and framing shops that provided materials and inspiration. But for the lengthy travel to UBC, we would have been happy to live our life here.

After Ken's birth I decided to venture into the 'fitness' era that had just begun to flourish. I went to an evening class and to my chagrin, was assessed as being entirely flabby and without good muscle tone. Surely all that intensive baby and toddler care would have kept me fit! Well, I decided to bite the bullet and began running around the Winskill Park playing field. Of course, I was soon out of breath and was forced to concur that I was anything but fit. I have become more fit over time.

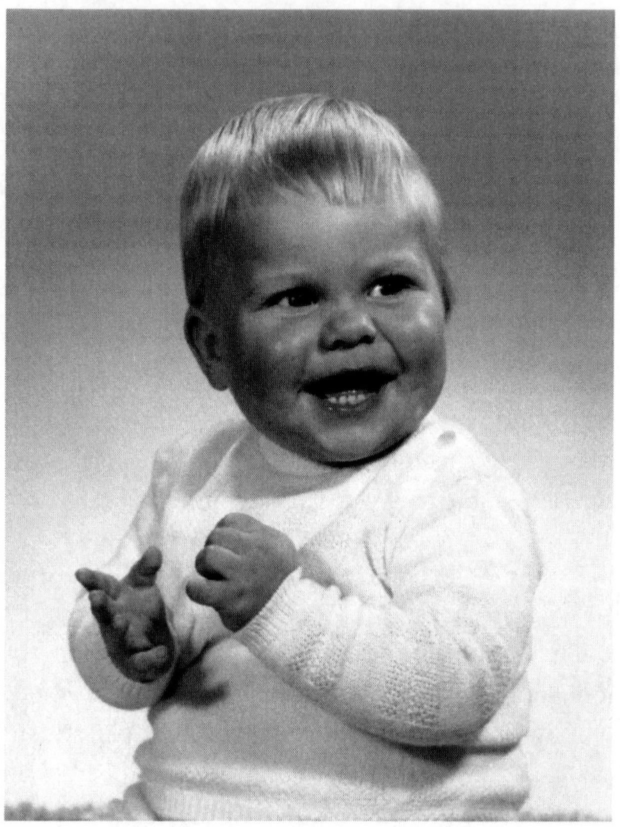

Kenneth Bradley Friesen, born on Dec. 11, 1966 in the Grace Hospital, Vancouver.

The family is complete. The children pose on Ken's first birthday in December 1967.

Southlands

The forest in the greenbelt between the city of Vancouver and the Musqueam Reserve is a hidden gem, crisscrossed by walking trails and bisected by a wandering stream. Our boys would find the droppings of feathers and bones under the trees in the forest left by the owls during their nightly hunts. The Southlands flats, home of some five hundred horses on acreages were close by and provided an exciting rural experience in the middle of a city. There was a horse trail that led through the park to the endowment lands. A wonderful walking trail led down to the Fraser River and followed the banks of the river on the edge of Musqueam Golf Club, Point Grey Golf Club and the Marine Drive Golf Club. The north arm of the river was a route for barges pulling sawdust; tugs pushing log booms to mills and pleasure boats. Salmon fishing at the mouth of the Fraser occurred in season. Across the water, the airport and its noise became an ever more noticeable neighbour.

We had come back to our old neighborhood where we first made our home in Vancouver in 1960. Holland Street is right next to Crown Street where we made our first home. When we moved back to Holland Street in Vancouver from Tsawwassen, the neighborhood still had some rural elements. Pheasants strolled across our yard. Hawks circled in the park. Our neighbors had a pen of exotic chickens in their backyard. The morning cacophony of birds and chickens was something we had to get used to. From our bedroom window we had a view west into the park that formed a greenbelt between the Musqueam Reserve and the city of

Vancouver. In the morning, the herons stopped briefly on the treetops before they flew off to their hidden home in the University Endowment forest.

Holland Street, below Marine Drive, is one long block, and in the early 1970's had some forty-two children under the age of twelve. To get to Southlands School, it was necessary to cross the busy Marine Drive traffic corridor. There was no thought of driving the children to school. It was safe enough for them to go on their own as long as they paid attention to the signals. It was a comfortable neighborhood. Activities and celebrations organized by individuals for the neighborhood occurred spontaneously. For special events the parents planned ahead Halloween was celebrated with fireworks in the park and goodies in someone's home afterwards.

John was happy to be close to the campus of UBC. He became immersed in the demands of his profession. In addition to teaching, he was required to be engaged in professional service to the community. He became president of the B.C. Council of the Family. He taught weekend and evening classes in outlying communities of British Columbia. He engaged in program evaluations such as the educational programs in the prisons across Canada.

We began to attend international conferences on a semi-annual or annual basis. We were fortunate to travel to many parts of the world such as England, France, Germany, Italy, Norway, Greece, Israel and to all major cities in the USA attending the American Association of Psychologists conferences and The International Round Table on Counseling. I usually went with John and found these events highly stimulating as well as relaxing. It was great to attend events featuring prominent writers, attend banquets with other professionals who became friends over time or just to indulge in some down time in a hotel. Of course these events afforded some prime shopping opportunities.

After settling into our home, in 1973, John arranged an exchange with Dr. Pierre Turgeon at the University of Ottawa. John taught summer school sessions at his University and Pierre taught courses at UBC. We exchanged homes for two months.

After a trek across Canada we arrived in Ottawa just in time for the July 1st celebration of Canada Day on the grounds of the Parliament buildings. Trudeau had been reelected as Prime Minister and parliament was in session that summer. We managed a visit to see it in action. Ottawa offered a great deal of inexpensive entertainment during the summer. We saw the RCMP Musical Ride free twice. Many plays were performed in the parks. The opera and symphony at the National Arts Centre were very inexpensive. We had intended to learn some French but it didn't happen. Ottawa's humidity kept the children indoors, except for swimming and other recreation. The violins had been brought with us, but practicing in such humid weather was too much of an effort.

When John finished lectures on Friday noon we would take off for the many attractions that were not far away such as Quebec City, Montreal, Toronto, Niagara Falls, Upper Canada Village and the like. My sister Lydia joined us and we left for the Maritimes without John in August. We had made a point of visiting all the legislative buildings across Canada. When we got to Halifax on a Saturday, we were told that the building was not open for viewing on Saturday. Before we turned away, a gentleman with a huge ring of keys appeared and gave us a private tour that included the CD Howe library that was usually off limits. He magnanimously ignored the usual red tasseled rope that kept tourists from wandering at will. In fact, he invited the children to test the speaker's chair offering them their choice of top hats from the cupboard where they were kept for the elected speakers on their formal occasions.

It was the granite steps that are at the entry to the Prince Edward Island Legislature in Charlottetown that caught our attention. The stones had a rounded indentation from years of wear and gave us a sense of history. The island was a favorite in its rural simplicity. The lobster supper in a church basement, the Anne of Green Gables homestead and the pleasant shoreline made for an unforgettable experience. It was something just right for elementary school aged children.

Our next three summer vacations were spent on Gossip Island, a little island off the east coast of Galiano Island. We stayed in the waterfront home of Steve Marks, one of John's colleagues. The dry and rocky terrain, covered with Arbutus and evergreen growth, pungent grasses as well as salty ocean vistas gave us a sensual experience, both relaxing and stimulating. The tidal pools afforded endless interest for the children. Deer emerged from paths leading into the forest, unafraid of human presence. The sandy coves exposed to the sun during the day when the tide was out, provided a warm swim when the tide came in. There was nothing much to do but play, read and rest.

Gossip Island was our first exposure to life on the Gulf Islands. British Columbia and Washington State are fortunate to have this idyllic option so accessible. We have visited the San Juan Islands, which belong to the USA and enjoyed Friday Harbour, Roche Harbour and the open vistas of meadows, farming and fragrant lavender fields. This island was cleared of most of its forest growth and became a favoured area for early residents of the Pacific Northwest.

We have also enjoyed experiencing Savary Island. This flat island north of Vancouver, which takes approximately eight hours to reach by ferries, was the early alternative for the Hawaiian Islands and was extremely popular with Vancouver residents as a summer vacation destination. The Canadian Pacific coastal ships and Union Steamships scheduled Friday night departures from the inner harbour in Vancouver. This transport included an overnight cabin and white tablecloth dinner service. A Sunday night departure from Savary brought the workingmen back to Vancouver on Monday morning. Mothers with children generally spent most of their summer on the island. This island is particularly known and appreciated for its wide sandy beaches.

For Vancouver residents, Salt Spring, Mayne, Galiano and Pender Islands are very accessible. We have become particularly attached to South Pender Island where Ingrid and Ben have a lovely vacation home. John assisted them in having a very substantial house moved from Salt Spring by barge to Pender Island. It was a monumental undertaking. Fortunately, moving buildings has been in the Friesen DNA for many years. Pete Friesen John's brother has been dubbed the guru of the moving industry and has been the consultant on many of the most significant building moves in the USA including the Cape Hatteras Light House.

The Pender retreat is stunning. It took considerable effort to re-establish it. A full basement was built underneath the house before it was lowered to its position. A broad deck wraps the house on the ocean side. The very large living room is enclosed with glass windows up to the twenty-foot ceiling. Every room is unique and spacious. One can sit and watch the ocean tides ebb and flow. A quote found on the ferry makes the point well. " In time, water erodes everything, even boredom". This has been our experience on Pender – we often drop the books we are reading and just enjoy the view.

Gossip Island beach

Women's Liberation

In the seventies, with all the children in school, I began to experience a feeling of restlessness. I was always busy but not entirely satisfied with where I was in my life. The women's liberation movement was gaining steam and books and the press carried a constant stream of material on the issues facing women. Birth control was now an option to limit families. Women had the same opportunity to become educated as men. Modern labor saving inventions and a high standard of living resulted in other options besides homemaking being the sole preoccupation of women.

One November, I made five versions of gingerbread houses for Christmas and was featured at women's club meetings. It was really not my thing. John came home one day with the information that the Vancouver School Board was looking for a counselor at the Britannia High School to finish the term from January to June. I decided this was my opportunity and went for an interview. At the school board office, I was surprised to meet two of the teachers who had taught with me at Templeton who were now in administration. When I indicated my interest in the position, they said to the supervisor, "Hire her, she's pure gold." I got the job and a big ego boost as well. I enjoyed the term and the entry back into the working world.

Our various financial experiences had left me with the feeling that I needed to be much more informed about the business world. It seemed that John could never be content with his professional interests alone and always needed to dabble in business. I am not the kind of person to be satisfied to discover what we should have known after the fact. I like to consider all the options before, not after a commitment is made to a business deal. With the new openness to women in law, I saw my opportunity and decided to take the LSAT exam. I was not even aware that one could prepare for it so I wrote it on a Saturday without any preparation. My ability in English stood me in good stead and together with a good BA grade average I made it into law school.

The experience of studying law was exhilarating for me. After so many years as a teacher and mother, confining my activities to a somewhat narrow range of challenges, being in a world of ideas and analytical thought was absolutely stimulating. I have to admit that when I first went into the law library and checked out the books, they were anything but engaging and they did sent a cold shiver up my back. But law is an activity of the mind, of dialogue, of joint struggle to understand issues and concepts. I particularly enjoyed jurisprudence and wished more classes that grappled with the larger principles of law and philosophy would be on the curriculum. Nevertheless, the ordinary problems of life are often complicated enough.

Initially, I committed myself to only one year of law. If it were to work, I would continue. John helped me to set priorities. I decided to schedule my classes between 8:30 am and 3:30 pm so that I could drop the kids off at school and be home when they arrived. I would not touch my books until 8:30 pm after activities; dinner, music practice and homework were out of the way. Bedtime was eleven. Weekends, two to three hours on Saturday during the time I waited for the children while at Youth Orchestra practice and several hours on Sunday night was my limit. My aim was to pass; I did not aspire to obtain high marks. I did better than I expected. The crunch came in December and in April. During exam periods, I required extra study time and yet Christmas activities demanded attention to concerts, recitals, shopping, partying, etc., etc. April was similar with its many events. I did feel it was all too much at times. During the second year John was due for a sabbatical and the pressure was off for a year with his greater availability. It made it much more doable. With the last year in sight, I no longer doubted that I would be able to accomplish this goal.

Fortunately, the family grew into the new challenges. It was actually a good thing that greater participation was expected from the children in keeping the household functioning. Jobs were offered for payment. Two dollars for cleaning a bathroom, four dollars for vacuuming the living, dining room, hall and stairs, four dollars for cleaning the kitchen, two for each of the bedrooms, three for the family room and the whole house merited twenty dollars if someone needed the cash. Meals were scheduled, first to Ingrid, then eventually all family members including John so that five week days were taken care of and I took over the weekends and the shopping and planning for the week to be executed by the family. John often struggled under the loss of a 100% housekeeper and the comfort of having a Friday night dinner with friends at our house that we had become used to. But slowly he became more house proficient. We all adapted to the new demands.

It was necessary to Article to be able to practice law. The demands made on students by the big downtown firms were somewhat medieval in terms of time and commitment. It was not something I would consider. I was fortunate to get a position with a modest firm in Ladner that had reasonable expectations and hours. One the most important aspect of being a litigator was taught to me by Herb Ivens, who challenged me never to get emotionally out of control, either in anger or frustration when in a trial.

After I finished the year of articles, I began to look around for opportunities and before long one presented itself. I had many acquaintances in the Fraserview MB church in Richmond. At least sixteen were realtors in the new Block Bros office that opened on Granville Avenue near No. 3 Road. Many of them encouraged me to open an office in the building. One day I met Harold Epp in chambers in the New Westminster courthouse and went out for coffee with him. Harold had graduated a year before me and was practicing with a downtown firm. He had a PhD in English from Berkley, California and had found it difficult to get a job teaching at a University. We agreed to form a partnership and open a practice in Richmond.

The partnership proved to be most enriching in terms of relationships and compatibility. Over the years we engaged in discussions touching on philosophy, religion, politics, literature and law. Our ethnic background and similar religious backgrounds allowed us to explore, without reluctance, the experiences life presented to us.

In 1978 my father died. When the telephone call came on a Sunday morning that he had died in his sleep, I experienced a sudden and sharp pain in my chest. He had been ill for several weeks and hospitalized after he and mother returned from their trip to Alberta. It became evident to me when we visited him at home on the Wednesday before, that he knew he was dying. I could read it in his eyes. There was a mixture of sadness and resignation when he looked at me. I felt like saying something about this feeling but was unable to do so. When a parent dies, he does not leave your consciousness. Thoughts of my parents come to me frequently. I had always had a good relationship with my father and he had always been supportive of me in my undertakings. His enthusiasm for life was a particular legacy that he left to inspire us, his children.

His death was devastating for my mother. His wellbeing had always been the central concern of her life ever since he became ill with diabetes at the age of thirty. Now she seemed to lose her reason for living. The fact that she had ten children and many grandchildren could not fill the gap left by father. The years after his death were not happy for her. Her declining health added to the problems. Most of all, as a woman who had never done any banking, nor had she learned to drive a car, so her life became very different than when she could rely on father to provide such amenities for her.

The mother we knew was always a strong person. She grew up in the home of a schoolteacher but was not permitted to go beyond the eighth grade. In the Russian north where she lived during her teen years, the girls were required to do the farm work while the sons, if they were so inclined could pursue secondary education and even go beyond that. She was a tireless worker and loved the challenges of home and family. During the depression, she sewed most of our clothing, including our coats from clothing discarded by others. She maintained her family of ten in good clothing and in clean clothing no matter what her circumstances. Her ability to cook and bake was without equal. Her six sons who did her food more than justice particularly appreciated brown and white bread, buns, cookies, cakes and special ethnic delicacies. She never had time to read books to us and since English was not her first language, she left education to the teachers. She had no difficulty speaking English and reading the newspaper. Father was one to constantly expand his vocabulary. Unfortunately, his children were often amused by his pronunciations and his attempts at sophisticated discussions on the telephone with English speaking professionals. He took his profession as a chicken farmer and hatchery operator seriously, joining the various cooperatives and associations that sought to improve productivity and poultry strains.

Our parents built a strong family. Throughout the years, in spite of the various paths we have taken, there has been a strong sense of family and togetherness. Christmas Celebrations on a yearly basis and picnics in the summer continue. As I grow older I am aware that even though we are siblings, we are very different from each other. This difference becomes more evident as we grow older, marry and develop our own family cultures. In part, this feeling of responsibility for each other is very much encouraged by the parents during the growing up years. The older siblings in the family are co-parents in many ways and it is a role no one encourages them to give up. This fact often creates problems as some in the family take it upon themselves to be critical of attitudes, beliefs and practices that are not conforming to what, in their opinion is appropriate for "our" family. Growth occurs when we give each other freedom to be and become what is right for each of us.

Our family at the time I had just started my law career. Samantha, our cat lived to the ripe age of 21 years and Dorie, our sheltie stayed with us for 8 years.

Profession of Law

The City of Richmond was a sleeper until the early eighties. It was a cheap and accessible bedroom community for Vancouver. Property values were low as the land protected by dykes was at flood level. Lulu Island was a convenient site for the Airport. The peat bogs and accreted soil provided attractive options for blueberry farms and produce production. Acreages were inexpensive. Fisherman, especially those of Japanese ancestry, dominated the Steveston area and made their living as fishermen. Light industry and forest product manufacture lined the two arms of the Fraser River shores. Substantial farming could be found in the central core. All of these factors continued but suddenly a huge surge of development flooded across the municipality as if a dyke had been ruptured. This development has continued unabated for two decades to the point where it has become a forest of residential low and high-rise development. It became the choice of residence for the Chinese immigrant population that now represents approximately sixty percent of its population.

In the early eighties, the economy went through an alarming spike. Housing prices soared. Interest rates went so high that businesses collapsed. Suddenly, the realtors who had been driving beautiful new cars and taking expensive vacations, were declaring bankruptcy. Our office alone handled at least fifty or more bankruptcies. Professionals such as doctors, lawyers and accountants had jumped on the bandwagon and invested in huge projects only to see their hard earned money evaporate. The pain of bankruptcy, the stress of dealing with bank debts resulting from failed investments became a heavy burden on just about everyone and the effect on marriages, mental health and the family stability was devastating. Much can be attributed to a monetary policy that was unresponsive to the economic forces and the failure of the government to control interest rates. We had become a silent partner with John's brother, Bill. John and Bill were building condominiums and houses in Burnaby and Surrey. During this crunch we, too, lost all our accumulated profits and savings. What we had left was our home and our incomes. That was a lot under the circumstances. We gave up our aggressive approach for a couple of years.

Becoming a competent lawyer takes a lot of blood, sweat, and tears and a lot of time. There is a lot to learn in the casebooks and the textbooks. Reading and analyzing information takes a lot of time and diligence. The process of establishing precedent on issues of law is an honored tradition in the English Common Law that governs the legal system in Canada except in the province of Quebec where the Civil Code governs. As with all common law countries, Canadian law follows the doctrine of *stare decisis.* Lower courts must follow the decisions of higher courts by which they are bound. All British Columbia lower courts are bound by the decisions of the British Columbia Court of Appeal. Only the Supreme Court of Canada has the authority to bind all courts in the country with a single ruling. The busier courts, such as the Court of Appeal for Ontario, for example, are often looked to for guidance on many local matters outside the province, especially in matters such as evidence and criminal law. However, the Ontario Court of Appeal does not bind the British Columbia Court of Appeal, but such decisions are often considered *persuasive.*

For historical reasons, Quebec has a hybrid legal system. Private law follows the civil law tradition of France, which was codified in the Civil Code of Quebec, a general law that contains all the basic provisions that govern life in society, namely the relationships among citizens and the relationship between people and property. Legislation enacted by the provincial legislature in matters of public law, such as the Code of Penal Procedure, should be interpreted following the common law tradition. It has also incorporated the Human Rights provisions in fairly recent revisions. Likewise, legislation enacted by the federal parliament in matters of private law, such as the Divorce Act, is to be interpreted following the civil law tradition and in harmony with the Civil Code of Quebec.

Family law is emotionally demanding. I got into family law for various reasons. John had a private counseling practice for years, which included many marital situations. I had also been a girl's counselor in the Vancouver High Schools. The third factor was that in addition to the solicitor type of work, I took on some Legal Aid cases during the first years of practice. There were many divorce cases offered by Legal Aid. I learned very quickly that these cases required a lot of management. The first mistake I made was to give clients my home telephone number. After receiving phone calls at two in the morning from clients engaged in a quarrel with their spouses, I kept my home number off the record.

Court work has high drama and tedious work. Every case that actually goes to trial has gone through many phases of exploration and attempted settlement. Most of the work is done in the office. Information is gathered through personal interviews of the client. Issues are recognized. Interim problems are dealt with through letters and telephone calls. If there are no solutions agreed upon, applications are made to the court called chambers, for hearings and interim decisions on individual matters. If the lawyers agree, settlement conferences can be productive. If all else fails, the matter is set for a trial.

Trials take every ounce of your focus and energy. The process requires that a thorough 'examination for discovery' be held where each party can be thoroughly examined by the opposing lawyer. This is a good time to find out the strengths and weaknesses of both your client's position and that of the opposing counsel. Often many documents are made available to support evidence of income, assets and other family information.

The next process is to sort through the evidence and then consider the precedents in law. Precedents determine how to treat the claims and expectations of the parties and reflect how the court has dealt with issues under similar situations. Arguments are then prepared to support the position you feel is appropriate for your client.

At trial, there is always the wild card of the witnesses. Witnesses are usually well prepared before going to trial, but they can often surprise you. At times, I have often dealt with the aspersion cast on lawyers "lawyers are liars', but not infrequently I have found that witnesses can be the worst liars. I think that this is prompted by their desire to save their skin or their money.

Are trials a struggle between right and wrong? Truth is a very significant question in law. There are, however, many other factors that make it less black and white. This becomes most evident in a trial. It is not until every witness has been heard that a more complete picture of the "truth' emerges. Every person has perceptions, biases, filters, etc. through which situations are seen or judged. Memory is at most, partial for most people. If you ask a half-dozen witnesses to a car accident to recount what they saw, their perceptions will often have much in common, but also have many differences.

Justice is blind. The traditional visual symbol of "Justice" is a blindfolded woman holding a scale and a sword. The scales are for weighing right and wrong; the sword is to punish the guilty; the blindfold is to show that she is impartial (that she does not treat friends differently from strangers, or high ranking people better than humble ones, because she does not see them). But she is not deaf, because she listens to all the evidence put before her. It doesn't matter who you are, what you look like, what race you are, if you are rich or poor – justice does not see that. Justice is equal to all. At the Law Courts in Vancouver, we have such a statue in the atrium.

Even your 'enemy' or adversary in court can be a good companion out of court. One of the attitudes in the legal culture is that in a good court setting, a lawyer does not allow his personal emotions to become identified with that of the client nor does a competent lawyer ascribe to the opposing counsel the burden of the case being litigated. In representing a client, it is very important to give the best advocacy, to be forceful, fearless and even sometimes to argue fiercely for your client. This does not mean that after that has been done, that a collegial and generous response to opposing counsel cannot be maintained.

Respect is essential. The tradition of law has an excellent tradition of civility. Unfortunately, the law profession has become less civil over the last few decades. There seems to be a move to "hardball" litigation, which involves the use of tactics of anger, intimidation rather than a civil, ethical, and humane approach. There are of course often conflicting expectations and demands, and the often confusing roles between advocating fiercely and problem solving, leading to a great deal of stress being placed on lawyers to do what is right and best under the circumstances. The tension between being civil and being a forceful and fierce advocate is one more stress added to the many other aspects of the legal profession that causes stress – pressure of billable hours; pressure to collect fees; long hours; the detailed and exacting nature of our work accompanied by severe consequences if performed otherwise. Then lawyers often deal with conflicted and emotionally disturbed clients and files which often involve the most troubling of human emotions.

To alleviate stress and maintain civility, it is important to maintain courtesy and show respect for fellow lawyers, for the profession, for clients and for yourself. It is possible to school oneself in the use of kindness in the face of rudeness, humour in response to anger, gentleness in response to anger and above all, self-control.

Sea to Sky

In 1985, John and I spent a long weekend in October in Whistler. The weather was warm and serene. The scenery was breathtaking. We were so overwhelmed by the beauty of the resort; we decided that this was where we would invest in a chalet for our children and ourselves. When we were still living in Tsawwassen, we had started skiing under the lights on Seymour Mountain on Friday nights. By the time the kids were teenagers, we were going to Mt Baker, to Manning Park and even to Banff. It appeared that this would be a good family activity for at least the next ten fifteen years. In the fall of 1985 we were ready to purchase a lot.

We had no trouble finding a lot in Whistler Cay Heights. We decided to buy a duplex lot, build it out and sell one side so we could afford the other side. We had less than ten thousand dollars to start the project plus borrowing potential. This meant that we would have to be very careful on costs and that we would have to do a lot of the work ourselves. We had seen a house plan in Whistler that we loved. We found out that the architect who had designed the house lived on Dunbar Street in Vancouver. We met with him and he gave us the plans and permission to adapt them to duplex structures. There was little or no activity in Whistler when we started to build. Weekend after weekend we rushed about hiring a framer, supervising the pouring of the foundations, purchasing lumber and generally supervising the project. We were our own contractors.

The building project was very challenging. Going to Whistler on weekends after a busy workweek is a change and not necessarily a negative experience. We had also been our own contractors in the building of our house on Holland Street so we felt confident in our ability to manage this project.

But our limitations were time. In June we left the framer to his own devices as John and I attended a Conference in Jerusalem where he was scheduled to present a paper at an International conference. We took our usual approach maximizing the enjoyment of this trip by adding ten days in Greece to the ten days in Israel.

On our way to Jerusalem, we first visited Athens, the beautiful Parthenon and the Agora. The weather was very comfortable in June and the Mediterranean Sea, a stunning blue. We had scheduled flights on the Olympic Airlines to the islands of Cyprus, Santorini and Crete. Unfortunately, the Olympic Airlines chose to be on strike during our vacation.

We quickly accepted the alternative of using the ferry system to find an island retreat. We found a resort on the Island of Egeda, which provided accommodation and food for the meager sum of two hundred dollars for one full week. This resort was a favorite of the Germans and the Danes. All the waiters spoke German so we had no language difficulties. The highlight of this beach vacation was that the European women preferred to sunbath topless. This was a novelty for both John and me, to say the least, having regard to our conservative upbringing.

We then went to Israel for the conference on family therapy. While John was engaged with the conference, where he presented a paper on anorexia, I had the luxury of walking about Jerusalem on my own. That was difficult enough, as I constantly had to decline the offers of individuals offering themselves as my guide. I enjoyed Old Jerusalem's busy streets and visited the usual tourist sites. The Hadassah Hospital is not near the centre of Jerusalem and I took an hour's drive on the city bus to reach it. The stained glass windows of the twelve tribes of Israel by Marc Chagall as well as the table weavings were a visual feast. I had seen his stained glass window at the United Nations building previously. And this was an opportunity not to be missed.

After the conference, John and I together with one of his colleagues rented a car. We drove to Bethlehem first where we visited the Church of the Nativity. It was a beautiful experience for me. A group of German pilgrims led by a priest were just singing beautiful carols in German and moving down the underground walkway to the site thought to be the birthplace of Jesus. When we arrived, the priest read the Luke Chapter Two passage. It was an extremely moving experience for me, especially because the voice of the priest reminded me so strongly of that of my grandfather, Peter Suderman. My first Christmas experience had been at the grand parents home in Dunrea, Manitoba with the scripture being read by my grandfather beside a candle lit Christmas tree.

We continued our travels to Masada, the ancient fortress near the Dead Sea. The guide gave us a thorough historical background to the resistance stand of the Jewish remnant that fled Jerusalem to Masada to the fortress where they held out for three years. They were surrounded by Roman troops who finally constructed battering rams and catapults to breach the fortress. Once it became apparent that they would soon succeed, the leader of the revolt, Eleazar ben Yair made a speech and convinced the defenders that they should never be the servants of the Romans and that it was preferable to die bravely and in a state of freedom. It is against Jewish law to commit suicide, nevertheless, it was better that their wives should not be abused and their children become slaves. All except two women with five children who hid themselves committed suicide. The famous writer, Josephus, recorded this part of history. He apparently got his information from the women.

Not to be missed was a swim in the Dead Sea, and yes, it was easy to float effortlessly. We stayed overnight in a Kibbutz nearby. Interestingly, there were a lot of former East European Jewish guests. Somehow, there are a lot of traits that are common to Mennonite people and Jewish people.

The next morning we continued towards Jericho and passed without incident. The day after, we learned that rocks had been thrown at a tourist vehicle on the previous day. We spent some time in the area of the Sea of Galilee. My feeling was that the climate is very similar to that of Hawaii and I was not surprised that Jesus and his disciples spent a lot of time here. We had Peter's fish for dinner. The hill where Jesus delivered the Sermon on the Mount was, again, a very meaningful experience. So much is part of my subconscious when I visit these memorable sites in the land of Palestine. The map of Palestine in the Bible was the first map that I ever studied.

We visited Nazareth and then Tel Aviv. A long walk on the shore of Mediterranean before bedtime exhausted us but gave us a time to observe the local people. Then it was back to Jerusalem and a four-hour security check before we were allowed to board our return flight. As our plane taxied on the runway, armored vehicles flanked both sides of the plane until takeoff. The reason for the excessive security was the response to the high jacking incident on board the cruise ship, MS Achille Lauro, in October 1985. Four heavily armed Palestinian terrorists demanded the release of fifty Palestinian prisoners. They killed a disabled American tourist, Leon Klinghoffer, and threw his body overboard together with his wheelchair. For this reason, there were very few tourists visiting Israel during this time.

We returned home and to our building site in Whistler with some trepidation and concern. Our fears were fully realized. Not only had our framer disappeared, but he had not paid his carpenters and liens were registered against the property. I spent considerable time and effort to sort out the mess. Learning by doing has its rewards.

We persevered and our duplex moved on to the next stages. John hired one of his graduate students who also had building experience to construct the windows in our Vancouver garage.

One lovely Saturday morning, the windows were loaded onto our trailer and John drove the station wagon pulling the trailer to Whistler. He had just passed Horseshoe Bay when the vehicle ground to a halt. He barely managed to pull off the road. John, called me at home and I picked him up and took him to Budget Rentals where he rented a truck; the windows were loaded on to the truck and taken to Whistler. The station wagon met its demise. We phoned a wrecking company, who paid us the princely sum of one hundred dollars for the vehicle and removed it from the roadside.

The further undertaking of the 'student carpenter' was to put the cedar shakes on the roof. John did not adequately supervise the process and as a result, the performance of the roof left much to be desired over time. Eventually, we replaced the roof with a metal roof, which is a much more preferable type of roof in Whistler.

We used pine boards for the ceilings and some walls to create the cabin look. The family members were recruited to do the staining. The drywall hires were of dubious character and not altogether reliable. But amazingly, the drywall got done and was reasonably well done.

The plumber lived just up the street from us. He had a very nice house constructed on the old European style of post and beam. He was of great help and managed to connect us with other trades, as they were required.

We did not have very much in funds so this enterprise required a lot of 'do it your self' work. I scoured the remnant shops for carpets and found amazing bargains. The challenge was to find color matches and quality. We did very well on both counts and the carpets lasted from twenty to twenty-two years with a great deal of rental traffic to deal with throughout their life span. In 1986, bargains were very much available as the housing market had taken such a heavy beating during the early eighties and had not yet recovered.

Finally, we completed the building by the middle of November. The carpet had been laid out and cut in the cul-de-sac and installed on the 15th, and the first snow fell on the 16th of November. We had intended to sell one side. We put up a 'For Sale" sign. Immediately, we inquiries about rentals and we were able to rent both sides at a very good price. On one side, a gold mining company executive rented the premises. We carefully asked if he would be open to pay the rent for one year up front if we gave him a considerable discount. This he did happily enough and so we could pay off the remaining trades that were not covered by the mortgage proceeds. To our astonishment, he said we could use it whenever he was not going to use it. We were able to use it rather frequently as he was a busy man.

Over the years, we had many excellent tenants. Many young people from Eastern Canada, Australia, New Zealand, Japan and even Greece found their way to Whistler. Some, of course, were not as they described themselves during their interview. John became adept at long chatty interviews where their real personas became evident and formed the basis of much better choices. We had the luxury of having at least a hundred calls for one advertisement, as rentals were scarce during the eighties and nineties.

Our family grew and Whistler became the 'family farm' alternative were adults and children can be together in an informal and prolonged periods. We now have twenty-two bodies and both sides of the duplex accommodate the gang. The Friesen grandchildren formed a whole ski class at times and thoroughly enjoyed the mountain together. Christmas holidays, Thanksgiving weekend, summer vacations were rarely missed. A canoe ride on Green Lake or Alta Lake or for a more thrilling adventure, down the River of Golden Dreams when the spring runoff was high added to the options.

Slowly, sports, school, church and other commitments were in competition for the weekend free time. Biking, particularly, mountain biking has become the passion of the big and little boys. For John and me, the quiet of a midweek break allows us to read, walk and generally enjoy the beauty of our mountain retreat, even as we have to give up the downhill skiing.

John and I pose for a photo on the top of Whistler Mountain. We always preferred Whistler runs to those on Blackcomb.

Ingrid, Maddie, Lexi, Izzy and Carolyn enjoying a good day on Whistler.

The Menno Simons Centre

There never was a busier year for us than 1986. This was Vancouver's Expo year. The whole city was engaged in the hosting of visitors and in celebrating the five months of festivities. We felt we had to be part of that as well and managed at least five visits. Our children were busily running a bed and breakfast in our basement suite. One of the performances at Expo, which we enjoyed, was that of k.d. lang, the 'wild rose from Alberta' who was just being noticed as a star. On stage with her as her songwriter, guitarist and producer was Ben Mink. It was to be our first introduction to our future son-in-law.

Expo provided Vancouver an opportunity to celebrate as a city. The financial management taken on by Jim Pattison ensured its success financially. The people owned the event, supporting the five-month party by their attendance and extravagant hospitality. The world came as our guests and as a city, we embraced the world. The beauty of British Columbia, labeled the province as being a supernatural province. After the first month of our usual rainy cool weather, unparalleled sunshine for the last four months, created a magical ambience for the event.

In 1986, our small Bible Study group interested in student ministry became aware of the sale of the Catholic Nun's Residence at 11th Avenue and Crown Street. We found this building to be what we had been looking for. We put in an offer of $ 605,000.00 and scrambled madly to raise the down payment. By September 1, we had purchased that building, retained the services of Walter and Janet Bergen as Residence Coordinators and rented the rooms to twenty-some students. The building was named the Menno Simons Centre. On the first Sunday in September, the first service of the Point Grey Fellowship was held in the chapel of the building, founding a new Mennonite church on the west side of Vancouver.

This project became central to our activities apart from our professions for the next twenty-five years. Our interest in student ministry was very much a part of our life. It became the mission of our congregation. Learning and higher education among Mennonites has had an uneven past. The early churches in British Columbia were largely rural. The move to Vancouver from the Fraser Valley from the fifties onward was job and employment oriented. However, many graduates of the Mennonite Educational Institute and other institutions also came to Vancouver for the purpose of gaining a University education. There was still a certain suspicion and fear among church leaders that a University education would take young people away from their traditions and particularly away from their faith. Most ministers did not have a university education. What was endorsed in the traditional Mennonite community and approved by them was Bible learning at Bible Colleges and Theological training at the denominational colleges.

The U. S. had established Tabor College, a Christian College as early as 1908. It offered graduate and undergraduate degrees. I was very disheartened when the decision was made by the Canadian Mennonite Brethren Conference to become partners and joint owners of the Seminary in Fresno. I had hoped that an institution would finally be established in Vancouver. What Vancouver has lacked to support the growth and development of the urban Mennonites and their churches, is an institution that would unite the various churches in a common undertaking. This would form a centre of thought and faith exploration in the urban context. Community has always been a very necessary component of faith building. This aspect has been totally absent in Vancouver. The Mennonite Brethren churches, in the past and presently operate in relative isolation from each other with little mutual support and interaction. An institution could have provided the focus to assist this process.

Also, over time, there has been an exodus of Mennonite people from pricey Vancouver to the suburbs of Surrey, Langley and the Fraser Valley generally and the Mennonite church presence has dwindled in Vancouver. The students in the Fraser Valley subsequently gave a great deal of support to Trinity Western University in Langley, even though it was not a denominational institution. Vancouver was abandoned by Mennonite Conference planning. This was the gap we perceived and sought to fill in a very small way.

The work at the Menno Simons Centre has been very rewarding and satisfying. It required a great deal of practical work improving, renovating and maintaining the facility. It required endless fund raising and promotion in the community. It challenged us to relate to young people and mentor them in so many ways.

We found creative ways to sponsor the encouragement and development of musical talents, by founding the Abendmusik Choir and a Concert Series of performances by young artists. These series reflected the high number of classical musicians who came to live at the Centre in order to study at the UBC's fine Music School. Students appreciated the opportunity to perform and the Society benefited in the fund raising aspect. Unfortunately, the change in worship styles in the Mennonite Brethren churches over the last several decades has resulted in a radical decline of interest in classical music training. As a result, we have far fewer music students. The specialties of engineering, medicine, law and medicine are now the main attraction to UBC. The colleges in the other cities of BC now offer most undergraduate courses.

Speakers such as John Howard Yoder and John B Toews were brought in by our Society to encourage dialogue on Anabaptist distinctives. We started very ambitiously, attempting to round out the offerings of the residence aside from community, nurture and a roof over their heads. It was difficult to sustain.

Our initial congregation at Point Grey Fellowship started very small with about a dozen members sitting a round a table. Slowly it grew. We did not follow a 'church growth' model. Rather, we attempted to find ways of meeting the needs of those who attended. Worship music indulged in the rich musical heritage of four-part singing, singing part of the Messiah to celebrate Advent, to invite students to play instruments or sing and generally to make the church an expression of all who attended.

A further emphasis was the congregation and its style of worship. We settled for a style of lay participation with speakers coming from within the congregation and or guest speakers from the community. Every service had a response and discussion time that often provided as much insight on issues as the sermon did. The goal of our congregation was to model openness to asking questions and finding answers to faith issues. In the course of time we have built a large alumni of students with whom we continue to feel connected.

Fortunately, Regent College was established a decade earlier. Our connection to Regent College has been significant. It is a non-denominational Theological Collage located on the UBC campus for the purpose of assisting graduate students to integrate faith with learning and living. We have benefited greatly form our association with this institution and many Regent College students have lived at the centre.

I became involved as a board member with Regent College in the late eighties. It was a stimulating and satisfying experience. The board met three times a year over a weekend. Board members were from all over Canada, the USA, and from many countries outside of America. The institution has had a strong role in strengthening the Christian understandings and had drawn many students from all parts of the world. The last two years of the nine years I served on the board, I served as chair. One of the board's major undertakings was to engage in strategic planning during the two years I served as the chair. Two professional advisors were retained to assist the representatives from the faculty, administration, board and students in the process. We spent twenty-one days all told and opened my eyes to the importance of having a vision and constantly adapting it to changing circumstances. Belatedly in life, I realized that I enjoyed administration.

Regent College is favorably situated on the campus of the University of British Columbia. It has a well-designed building and has recently acquired an excellent library as well as significant classroom and seminar space. Fortunately, it has strong support from its non-denominational community. It is renowned for its excellent faculty. Students come from all over the world to study here. It offers much of what is offered in a seminary but goes much beyond in emphasizing integration of theology with professions and the workplace. Foreign students from Asian countries feel comfortable in this institution as well as mature students who are looking for career changes and seeking a deeper understanding and meaning for their life in secular society.

The summer sessions as well as the many conferences provide short-term stimulation and training. These summer sessions are very well attended. Many Christians, who work full time in various professions, often spent one or two weeks taking classes as a period of revitalization and inspiration to there Christian walk.

The Menno Simons Centre

Family

Our children graduated from high school and moved on to the University. It never occurred to us to promote higher education. It was a given since both John and I had always desired it for ourselves and it was something they all chose to do of their own volition.

Norman, Cynthia, John, Carolyn, Ken, Ben, Ingrid, Erna, John and Julie dining at the Seasons in the Park on Little Mountain on our 50th Anniversary.

INGRID AND BEN

Ingrid took her first year at UBC in General Arts. She was well read, an artist and studies came easily for her. I remember her sitting on the floor beside her bed with books scattered about studying in a very relaxed fashion. She used her desk only when necessary. After the first year, she took a year off from studies to travel and attend a fall session at the

Capernwray Bible School near Sydney, Australia. During the spring term she traveled with friends to New Zealand, the Cook Islands, Fiji and other south Pacific destinations. She returned to improve her depleted bank account and went on to obtain her BA in Arts at UBC.

Isabel, Ben, Ingrid and Lucie.

Ingrid was an easy student with a creative mind and an excellent memory. She had a hard time deciding whether to go into Counseling/Psychology like her Dad or to go into Law like her mother. She decided to be a lawyer. She decided to study law Western University in London, Ontario. Ingrid finished her law degree at UBC, articled at Ladner Downs and became a prosecutor in the criminal system.

Ingrid met Ben Mink and has a happy marriage. Ben is both, an excellent musician and a wonderful human being. He has produced several CD's with k.d. lang and with many other groups and musicians. Ben and Ingrid have two girls, Isabel and Lucie. They live within seven minutes of our home.

CAROLYN AND NORMAN

Lexie, Norman, Ariane, Carolyn and Maddie Bishop.

Carolyn was the organized student. Her room was always in good order. It was not surprising that she decided to become a chartered accountant and a businesswoman. She always worked very diligently and went above and beyond the call of duty, even in her elementary school projects. She could always be relied on if she were given a task. She decided to study at Trinity Western University for her first University year. She then took a year for travel in Europe and returned to the University of B.C.

She took her courses in the Commerce Department. It was here that she met Norman Bishop who was pursuing a degree in Marketing. They fell in love and were married. Both of them found a career in Vancouver. Carolyn worked in various firms including an oil company but soon found her niche in the garment industry. Norm worked for food wholesale companies such as Oppenheimer Foods. Norman is a very talented promoter and salesperson. Before long, they, too, married and very quickly started their own business by purchasing the Symax Garment factory and business. They have stayed with this industry to the present day, expanding strongly into the US market. They have settled in Vancouver, within twelve minutes of our home. They have three girls, Madeleine, Alexandra and Ariane.

They have become aggressive in their marketing in the USA and have been successful in attracting such clients as Apple. It makes for a life of much travel, engaging in trade shows and connecting to agents in all major US cities.

JOHN AND JULIE

Joshie, Julie, Tessa, John and John Hayden posing on a log in Fairhaven where they live.

As a child, John loved to engage in conversation. He always needed to feel connected to his family and friends. This trait has stood him in good stead as he has spent much of his post-secondary education in the US. John had a gift for music, which was evident early on. He began as a violin student at five and very quickly decided that he preferred the cello. His studies took him first to UBC, then to Bloomington, Indiana for a year, Julliard, New York for two years where he obtained a Master's Degree and then to the University of Southern California in Los Angeles for three years where he obtained a Doctor of Music Performance. Phone calls helped to ease the separation form home and family.

He spent a few years playing with the Vancouver Symphony and playing as a solo performer. He joined a string quartet that toured in Japan for three months. He recorded four CD's and found that a solo career was very demanding in travel time. He accepted the opportunity to teach in Bellingham, at the University of Western Washington and has made his home there with Julie and their three children, Hayden, Joshua and Tessa. Julie has made his life complete. She is a trained nurse and a wonderful mother. Bellingham opened John's interest in business and he has been active in real estate in addition to developing a career as a professor and musician. With a Nexus card to assist in crossing the border into the US, we are able to visit with about an hour's drive.

KEN AND CYNTHIA

Ken learned by observing his siblings. He never was punished. He did not require it nor did we have the inclination, probably we had become better parents. He was also encouraged, he might say, required to grow up quickly. There were two reasons for this, the first being that he was to keep up with the older children and the second was precipitated by my decision to enter law school when he was in the second grade. Ken had a low voice and was often referred to as 'gravel voiced' Kenny in the neighborhood.

He too, went to UBC for a year, then to Capernwray in Kitzbuhl, Austria for the fall term. After the term, he traveled with several friends to France, Germany, Yugoslavia, Greece and England. The need to replenish his bank account brought him home for the summer. His stay in France was used as an opportunity to study French. He eventually expanded his French abilities by spending an exchange term at Laval in Quebec City during his law studies at Western

University in London, Ontario. After a year of Articles with Clark Wilson law firm, he became an associate and then a partner with Friesen & Epp.

Ken and Cynthia with their children, Charlotte, Samuel, Josephine and Isaac.

During his studies in London, Ontario, Ken enrolled in a French Immersion program in Trois Riverois for the summer months. This is where he met Cynthia, who was also in the program. Their romance began there and was culminated in marriage in her Chatham hometown later. We enjoyed eight years as neighbours on Holland Street where they still make their home. Cynthia is a wonderful mother to Charlotte, Samuel, Josephine and Isaac.

Time to Play

The desert sun is warm and caressing. Golf greens are deep emerald with cacti in the sand instead of green rough grass as in the Pacific Northwest. Grey and mauve shadows outline the hills and mountains that cradle the valley floor of the Palm Springs and Coachella Valley area. It has the lush quality of an oasis, which it has become thanks to the water drawn from the artesian subterranean stores below the valley floor. Walls surround gated country club after country club that provide luxurious accommodation and private amenities to its owners and patrons. The privileges accrue to those who have the money to enjoy this paradise. To a large degree, it is enjoyed by the older generation, which now has the time and the means. Whereas in the past, it was mainly the Hollywood stars and the idle rich that enjoyed this paradise, a slice of the pie is now available to the multitude of retirees from across the colder northern states of the US and Canada who are able to access these pleasures by way of timeshares, trailers and even home purchases. Children and grandchildren are permitted short time periods away from their jobs and schooling and are inducted into the lifestyle by their parents.

The negatives of old age become visible in this congregation of the aged. The infirmities, the obesity, the limitations of mobility and activity, are a poignant side bar of this blissful existence. Health is just about everything, if not everything, once you move past the age of retirement. And so we come to renew ourselves, to recover the mobility of our joints, to lower the blood pressure, to strengthen the heart muscles and to rest in the warmth of the sun rather than to struggle with the elements and endure the cold of winter.

But paradise is not limited to California. Maui is another grand Garden of Eden. Here the eternal beauty of the ocean enhances the warmth of the sun. Mesmerizing waves wash the sand and the sea is a symphony of activity and sounds lulling one to sleep at night and relaxing the feverish mind into a coma of rest during the day. One feels enveloped in a womb of warmth creating an aura of bliss. Zephyrs of wind caress the tanning body in nature's unsolicited massage. The beach is a source of joy as is the surf – so physical in its immediacy and intimacy. Both young and old enter into play. Play, that is restorative and mindless in its demands. Rest upon rest becomes a way of life and a happy experience of time – time, which loses its usual demands on us. A reminder of the passing of another day is marked by the blowing of the conch as the sun touches the horizon. Thus ends another day.

When the trade wind zephyrs give way to the strong winds of winter, the surf becomes ominous, washing away the sands from the far flung beaches, scouring the lava rock until little remains of the languorous cover of sand and baring the sharp protrusions that threaten the unwary footstep. Clouds roll in and obscure the blue sky, cloak the volcanic cones with swirling mists and interrupt the day with downpours. There is nothing left to do but huddle indoors with a good book or escape to the ubiquitous Wailea Mall to while away the time. Television is the entertainment or opiate of the aged and the infirm as well as of the indolent. The young are challenged by the rising surf and find every new beach that provides the ultimate ride of the curling waves. The contrast is sharp.

Time is suddenly available for conversation and reflection. There is significant perspective to be gained by removing oneself from one's usual preoccupations. Urgency recedes. A calm evaluation of life's issues is possible. New insights surface and present themselves. It is as if when one stops pushing at life, it starts to show itself for what is. It becomes easier to accept the challenges that emerge than to insist on overcoming them. Perhaps this is the most challenging part of the aging process – to learn to accept what we cannot change. The truly frightening aspect is that there are continual changes that mark this stage of life, for some constant and difficult and for others, gradual and hardly noticeable. Like the weather, life at this stage, is unpredictable.

At age seventy-five, John wakes up with a sore back on a February Tuesday morning in Maui after a Monday golf game. Slowly and gingerly he positions his body before he attempts a careful and slow move to an upright position. The back becomes the overriding concern for the next two weeks; Devils claw ointment is prescribed by a natural remedies acquaintance and applied liberally with little or no beneficial results. One noticeable result is an unintended one. John makes a nick with his razor on his chin and his blood seems to have thinned to the point where he finds it difficult to stop the bleeding. It seems time is the ultimate healer and his back slowly recovers, but not enough to risk another golf game, at least for now.

I have had tightness in my right knee since June of 06 and know it may have something to do with an earlier ski injury. Over time, tightness becomes swelling and I visit my doctor who says that I now have osteoarthritis in my knee. I don't want to accept his diagnosis and think some surgical procedure can be used to restore adequate functioning. However, when I finally give up my resistance to taking medications and take the anti-inflammatory drugs he has prescribed, the pain and swelling subsides and I have to admit that he was right. Arthritis, the scourge of the elderly is my lot as well. This means a limitation has now been imposed on our morning and evening barefoot walks on Keawakapu beach. If I am going to walk on the beach, I must at least wear shoes that give me good support as I already have inserts for a fallen metatarsal arch. For me, limitations are not easily accepted, but one has to face the reality of compromise.

So what is the "integration phase" of life all about? This period in life is about discovering that one is woefully uneducated. I have begun to read again, which means I am trying to keep up with current thought. That alone is a difficult task, especially when one stands in front of the explosion of options in a bookstore or follows the weekly recommendations in the Globe and Mail or other publication and is confronted by choice upon choice.

I am aware that I have neglected the classics, finally discovering Erasmus and his influence on the pacifist stance of the Mennonites. I am aware of the influence of the discovery of printing on the dissemination of knowledge at the beginning of the 16th Century. I have never read Dante's Inferno until this year. I read it lounging on a chair under Palm trees in Maui. I have vague notions of Philosophy, but must now read Kierkegaard, etc. I am theologically illiterate even though I have served on the board of Regent College for nine years and as chair for two years. John and I attend conferences to be stimulated and informed, a C.S.Lewis Conference in Oxford and Cambridge, a Bonhoeffer Tour sponsored by Wilfred Laurier and the University of Toronto. We buy book after book on various German theologians such as Karl Barth. We are astonished to discover a wealth of current American theologians as well as a solid foundation of theology, not only in Jonathan Edwards and his contemporaries. Stanley Hauerwas is recognized as a kindred spirit.

The recognition of lacking in understanding, acknowledging missed opportunities, regretting failures, rejoicing about unmerited blessings, confirming ones accomplishments, grasping for opportunities that remain and sometimes wishing one could do it all over again. It involves regretting the loss of youthful vigor, accepting what cannot be changed and maintaining the joy of living in spite of the challenges of diminished earnings, failing strength and more than anything, a greater uncertainty about the future. On the other hand, there can be certain recklessness in seizing the day and its opportunities. That of course, is the challenge.

The age of the computer and Internet, the cell phone the opportunities and challenges for the aging mind are numbing. Not only is our past technical learning not to be relied on, but also there is so much more to learn and learn and learn! There are simplifications but when my glasses tend to slip off my nose when I bend down to "read the instructions" on my DVD player, attach the myriad of plug ins on the TV, patience and perseverance are the required learning challenge of the day. It is wonderful to be able to take the laptop with you as you travel, but it is often a frustrating challenge to find the right technical port and mechanical device to accommodate the task.

The cell phone is another instrument of doubtful utility. It adds layers of busyness and frustrations, not to mention costs. On our very first car trip with the phone to Palm Desert, I cheerfully locate a motel and booked it. The charges when they arrived were shocking! I was not too unhappy when the cell phone disappeared from our lodgings in Palm Desert. It was not soon replaced.

The Ipad2 that we received as a gift from our children is a much friendlier companion for the challenged mind. The happy lessons at the Apple store set one on a friendly path of usage. It has the potential to remain a cherished companion.

John, enjoying the morning walk on Keawakapu beach in Maui.

The lush growth of tropical paradise can be enjoyed half way up to the summit of Mount Haleakala.

The Grandchildren

Children and grandchildren provide the most significant entry for the aging to the unfolding world. One has the option of closing one's eyes to the changes that are occurring or one can simply engage actively in the emerging culture. Spending time with infants recalls and reaffirms the viability of life and the future of mankind. It calls forth a commitment to assisting and nourishing them in a way more profound than what we experienced as parents. As parents we did our best, but inexperience, lack of awareness and just plain ignorance or self-absorption left many scars. It is easier to learn to understand contemporary culture through the eyes of a child than through the media or other options, and the best way is to "hang out" with the grandkids. The amazing result is that we begin to see the world through their eyes rather than through our own fossilized point of view.

Each of our twelve grandchildren is a new experience and a new gene pool of profound difference. They present a significant element of play in our lives. We have the advantage of living in close proximity to our children and grandchildren ranging from next door in the case of one family, seven minutes by car to two families and an hour to the fourth family. Living in the same community, allows the children to engage in sports together, visit frequently and to know each other almost as well as siblings. They go to camp together in summer, ski together in winter and frequently holiday together and with us.

Whistler has been the "family farm" component for our family. We spent so much time there with the four families when their children were infants and became older. Sadly, school and sports activities eventually claimed more and more of their time. Weekend soccer, and grass hockey were the most time consuming. Nevertheless, weekends continued to be a time of coming together, even though it was often limited to Friday and Saturday as Sunday was usually church day.

Maddie, the oldest is the pack leader. This leadership quality is not related to her age but her instinctual ability to determine what might challenge, entertain or interest the pack. The response of her siblings and cousins is not only unquestioning compliance and support, but also delighted engagement. She seems to gauge correctly what might be the ultimate activity or adventure. As she became a teen, and her interests were engaged with her peers, her leadership was mourned by the younger cousins.

Isabel is the scholar, poet, thinker and artist. Her thoughts are long and deep. Her sense of order, desire for achievement and persistence in pursuit of her goals results in superb achievements. She can sketch and paint with ease and accomplishment. Her book of poetry is profound and beautifully illustrated. As a student she achieves at the highest level and stands at the top of her classes. She has a sense of personal deportment that seems innate as well as sophisticated. Ballet is a discipline that suits her body and spirit. Her participation and ability to perform in Beauty and the Beast was exhilarating.

Alexandra has a beautiful quiet spirit. She is a perfect companion. Gentle in her demeanor, she is nonetheless the athlete with a strong competitive spirit and a strong and well-tuned body. She is capable and consistent in her academic achievements, in her music performance and in her daily activities. Reliability makes her an easy child to love. She has a spiritual quality and a faith dimension that is evident in her and draws friends to her circle. Lexi's 'Trek' program participation, as well as her training at the Pioneer Pacific Camp is reflective of her strong physical and mental abilities and interests.

Lucie is a happy and spirited child who takes on the role of being the peacemaker in the family circle. She is aware of others to such a degree that she thinks for them and is tuned to enhancing the experiences of all whatever they may be. She bounces through life literally and figuratively, cart wheeling, jumping from one position to the next in a joyous explosion of energy. Everyday is a happy day. When her energy is gone, she has the wisdom to go to bed and will disappear accordingly. Her ability as a dancer and performer reflect her gifts.

Charlotte is the perfect child. She cannot be faulted for anything. As the oldest child in her family, she is the model mother's helper. Her siblings adore her, trust her and accept her selfless love and concern. She is an inveterate reader and must be checked at bedtime to make sure she has given up her book for the night. This means that she is an excellent student and flourishes in the academic world. Piano first and then the harp are her instruments of choice. She has become the baker in the family and delights with her frequent and delicious desserts.

Ariane is the girl with the personal gift of fashion, sense of color and desire to enjoy the gift of beauty and comportment.

Her exacting need to find the right combinations and clothes for the occasion leads to frustration and challenge. On the other hand, she is a free spirit, strong of body and an athletic powerhouse. Her sociability requires that she maintain a wide circle of friends and playmates. She has been honored with the 'model' student award in her sixth grade.

Samuel, the first grandson, has had no difficulty in establishing his unique position as someone who does things and loves things that are masculine. He loves noisy equipment. He is a superb mountain biker, skier, soccer player and has considerable hockey talent. His academic competence allows him to enjoy a seemingly easy school achievement. He is also a collector of rocks, and enjoys all things that are mechanical and technically challenging. His inventive and curious mind is only one aspect of his strong academic performance and achievements. He is a favorite playmate of his girl cousins.

Josephine is a child that surprises with her uniqueness. She is not a follower and as the eighth grandchildren, it is not surprising that she has carved out her own path. She would have been happy to be an only child. She enjoys your full attention and thrives when she gets it. She is strongly motivated and will walk on a bed of coals if challenged, but it is she who will determine if that is what she wants to do. She has athletic competence built into her body. She is the best pianist in the family so far. Her care and attention for her family, especially for little brother Isaac, is the core of her existence.

Isaac, the renaissance cherub, has stolen all our hearts. His blond curls, his blue eyes and his genial nature evoke adoration and joy in all who surround him. His learning curve is astounding, taking up “hock” (hockey) at fifteen months, soccer at eighteen months, all of course participating with his siblings who cannot refuse him.

John Hayden is another cherub with blue eyes and blond hair as well as a ready smile. Blue eyes and blond hair, except for Madeleine, who has her father’s dark hair and brown eyes, and Ariane who has brown eyes; generally identify the Friesen clutch of grandchildren. The recessive blond gene has certainly made a strong showing. John Hayden, exuberant and happy is obsessed with the mechanical world of cars, trucks, buses and trains, not to mention all the other noisy wonders of industry.

Joshua has arrived to ensure a playmate for Hayden. He engages with a boisterous and sweet disposition. He is a “biker” beyond belief, riding a two-wheeled bike without training wheels before he reached his third birthday. He has the apt phrase and precocious insight that astounds his family and friends.

Lastly, John and Julia are blessed with the arrival of Tessa Jane. This child is fortunately or otherwise deemed to look like her mother, maternal and paternal grandmothers, which means she has brown, not blond hair. She has established herself as a calm, gentle spirit. The family celebrations have permitted the ‘let’s play with the babies’ option for the older girls for many years. Her grandfather Sauer calls her an angel, which her sweet temperament confirms.

Time changes everything and it is becoming evident that the teenagers are undergoing a profound change in activities, attitudes and physical growth. The current obsession with the Face book, Twitter, the chat rooms, the text messaging to friends, begins to dominate their leisure time. More and more, commitment to sports, dance, drama and friendships and boyfriends are defining their lifestyle.

As the four families mature, their particular family cultures become more distinct and differentiated. Suddenly, the easy relationships they had as small children at play take on a more challenging aspect. What is promoted in one family varies from that of another and it requires a wider acceptance as well as a more deliberate adjustment and acceptance of the other's difference. As our family meets formally and informally frequently, because we live within easy distance of each other, these are not temporary adjustments, but must be accommodated over the lifetime of the family unit.

This is the first batch of grandchildren. Back row, left Charlotte, Alexandra, Madeleine and Lucie. In the middle row are Isabel and Ariane. Samuel sits in front, the first grandson after six granddaughters.

The grandkids pose with us in June of 2010, the day we celebrated our 50th Wedding Anniversary. Tessa was born the next year.

The Best of Times, the Worst of Times

We are 'victims' of our own times and against our own understanding we are captive to the enthusiasms, preoccupations, current status and limitations of our knowledge and threats of our times. Our endowments, associates, restraints, supports, families, and political, economic, spiritual and religious environments limit or alternately enlarge our understandings.

As I consider the historical information available about the Suderman family in the historical sense, this fact becomes more and more evident to me. For this reason I have added a the following chapters which, include my father's story, my Mennonite family's community context in part, as well as historical research on the Suderman family that goes back to the 13th Century that has come to my attention through various sources. That there was a strong Suderman family in northern Germany that is documented in detail with genealogical charts was an astonishing discovery.

Our present age, particularly in America, is preoccupied with political and religious extremes. This was very much the case during the Middle Ages when the religious and political powers competed together and against each other for dominance. When I read and translated the dissertation and became familiar with the lives of these people, it astonished me how many of the ancient Sudermans were involved in the religious, political and economic life of the times.

Today, we suffer from a tendency to categorize and label, especially public and political thinking as either 'liberal' or 'conservative'. These labels, are, unfortunately, based on identifying sensitive issues and fail to take into account the variety of positions that constitute personal integrity. Such indices as religious belief, positions on social issues such as abortion, sexual practice are triggers for categorization rather than a balance assessment of an individual's composite position.

There is a failure in our present society to accept that each individual is entitled, even morally obligated to live out his or her religious or other convictions in society without denigration or rejection. It is said of Barack Obama that he has a gift for seamlessly weaving religious references into his language. This integrative perspective has been and is true for me. This is the perspective that has guided my life.

For example, it is inadequate to treat the worship in black churches as 'ethnic characteristics' rather than to understand how fundamental to their life these expressions are. It is not enough to limit religious references to 'safe' society if we are to live well-integrated lives.

In history, there have always been attempts by political, religious and social groups to control the thinking and behavior of others, directly or indirectly or by force. We have in the 20th century witnessed this in the Soviet Union as well as in Nazi Germany. Today we see the same horrors in the Arab countries and in North Korea. Sadly, even in families, differentiation is often never achieved or accepted. For me, it is an absolutely essential imperative that each person be permitted to live according to his or her convictions without censure, or even force or coercion.

After I retired from the practice of law, I engaged in an attempt to educate myself in my areas of deficiency, which are to say the least, numerous. I had been on the board of Regent College, a college that seeks to integrate theology and life for nine years and had little or no theological training. The attempt to continue to educate myself is like adding drops into a very empty bucket.

I was also on the board of the Canadian Mennonite University in Winnipeg for the first three years of its formation as a university. Recently, John and I have been actively engaged at the University of the Fraser Valley in the establishment of Peace Studies and a Centre of Mennonite Studies.

One area of interest for me was the concepts of the mind, the brain, the self, spirit and the soul in relation to the corporeal body. I had found definitions and explanations in writings of mystics; theologians, philosophers, scientists, psychologists, psychiatrists and medical practitioners lacked clarity or uniformity. There appears to be little basic definitional clarity on what the essence of the human spirit is.

To add to the complexity, we are now in the computer age and very new concepts of replacing the brain's functioning are becoming the norm. Creativity, invention, aesthetics, art, music and creative functions generally appear to be outside the scope of this artificial intelligence. The attempt to understand the soul and spirit, body and mind is an amazingly rich area of preoccupation that touches a broad area of understanding and intuition.

Reading has always been for me a door to the world. It has been enriching and rewarding to spend our retirement years in a University community, enhanced so significantly through our decade's long connection to the Regent Christian community at Regent College. Evening lectures of visiting scholars, the Laing Lecture Series and the amazing Library are endless sources of books and magazines.

Lectures and events at the University are frequent. The beautiful Chan Centre is so accessible for concert and other events. The Freddie Wood Theatre as well as the "Old" Auditorium and the Music school offer student and professional performances. The Botanical Gardens, the Japanese Gardens and the vast trails of spirit Park provide endless opportunity that only our personal limitations inhibit.

The concept of 'our being' in this world is, as the sciences reveal in concepts like quantum mechanics, relativity, the genome and DNA research is mind boggling. With the computer driven revelations and the tools of cyberspace adding to the knowledge pool, life seems more complex and irreducible than ever. The University now promotes itself as "A Place Of Mind".

The power of two persons living together in marriage is part of this final reflection. Each of us contributes to the other, both positively and negatively. John is a man of vision and enterprise. This quality was basic to his professional academic career. His contributions to family counseling and therapy were recognized at a conference in Oxford, England in 2003 where he received the Outstanding Contribution Award in Family Counseling

Apart from professional undertakings, there were many joint ventures during our lifetime. These were stimulated by our values, our needs and insights. Vision is a paramount quality. An undertaking can only succeed if there is a commitment to a vision. It must be nourished by inspiration, actualized by dogged determination, sustained by hard work and characterized by enthusiasm. My contribution in this process has been in some measure at all levels, but particularly by persevering when energy and enthusiasm waned.

We live our lives as they come to us. My reflections present an ordinary life. I consider the circumstances of life in Canada from the depression era during which I was born, to the present, a constantly improving trajectory economically and socially in the broadest sense possible. For our generation they have been 'the best of times'. My parents and their forebears faced different challenges and situations. My children and grandchildren live in a world that seems to be changing with even greater momentum and rapidity. Hopefully, they will also experience 'the best of times'.

Finally, my hope for the next generations is that in each of their lifetimes, they could experience that inner security and certainty that "in Him we live and move and have our being".

The Mexican Adventure

The following is an article that appeared in the "*Mennonite Weekly Review*" on June 16th, 1925. H. P Krehbiel wrote about the Mennonite emigration from Russia to Mexico. My father and his family together with a large group from his village arrived in Mexico from Russia in the same year in the same area, but later in the fall. He refers to the region as Irapuato whereas in my father's reference the name is referred to as Iraquato. Alf Siemens drew this article to my attention.

One wonders why the Mennonites would have risked going to Mexico in that they were attempting to escape the Russian Communist Revolution. There was a similar struggle in Mexico with forces attempting to create a Communist government at that time.

A GLIMPSE INTO OLD MEXICO
(As written by H. P. Krehbiel)

Some of the Mennonites who have come from Russia to Mexico within the last twelve months have located in central Mexico. The place where they have located is Irapuato, in the state of Guanajuato. The town of Irapuato lies just beyond Silao, the place last mentioned in the preceding paragraph. The Mexican National Railroad, on which I was traveling runs generally south until it reaches Irapuato, there it joins the transcontinental road running east and west. Accordingly, this city is an important railroad center, with a population of about thirty thousand.

This was Easter Day. Unfortunately, our train was late which brought me into Irapuato at ten o'clock instead of seven-thirty in the morning. During the few days that I had now spent in Mexico, my vocabulary in Spanish had been increased a little, however, contemplating that I should make the Mexicans understand that I wanted to be taken to the Hacienda Las Animas made me feel quite uncertain about the outcome. But when we reached the station, Mr. Patton, an American who had spent more than thirty years in Mexico and with whom I had been traveling since leaving El Paso two and one half days ago, got off the train with me and in a few moments had told them what I wanted, and he offered himself to be my guide.

Within two minutes, I was in an antiquated carriage without a top drawn by two mules, and off we were for Las Animas. I was in the company of two native Mexicans, who were total strangers. They could not understand me and I could not understand them. I wondered where they would take me. We rattled away over the antiquated cobblestone street for several blocks, then through some side streets until we got into the open, when the driver turned his mules down the excavation alongside the railroad track, where there was no sign of any road and to the side of which was simply the lonely open country. This would be the sort of situation into which U.S. bandits would like to get a stranger if they intended to waylay him. But nothing evil has happened to me at the hands of those sons of Aztecs. Shortly, we entered a well-driven road and very soon we were on the Hacienda Las Animas.

A hacienda is simply a very large farm. Las Animas has about 2000 acres. The custom was to have the buildings located somewhere near the center of the farm. This is also the case on Las Animas. The place has been in a neglected condition for some years, as a result of the revolution. Yet, even so, the large buildings and equipment impress one that things were formerly done on a large scale. In the house, now partly in ruins, which might have been considered a mansion in its better days, there is room for a number of families. Three families were living in it when I was there, and they had ample room. Large barns and cattle sheds were on the place. The former owner had Mexican families on the place to do his work for him. A number of these families still lived there, and were working some of the land against a rental. The Mexicans had some cattle, which they were herding on the pastureland. These people were living in small huts along the outside walls of the buildings.

Aaron Rempel, a man of seventy years, who had been in Mexico for more than two years, was instrumental in completing this purchase from the Mexican Land Treasury. As we walked up to the house, he was sitting in the shade of the house quietly resting. A most cordial reception was accorded me. I soon learned that everyone had gone over to the other hacienda, St Juan, where another group of Mennonites is located. It was soon decided that, after a brief survey of the surroundings and a simple meal, we too, would go over to St Juan. This we did afoot, for it is only about two miles from Las Animas to St Juan. The trip led up through the middle of the town and right through the market place and streets. In the streets women and children were selling a variety of wares, particularly plentiful was pottery. These Mexicans seem to excel in making all sorts of crockery, both large and small. We also walked about in a large market building were selling was proceeding even though it was Easter Day – the same as any other day. Hundreds of people were busily engaged in buying. Irapuato is an old town, many of its buildings dating back hundreds of years. The streets are narrow, and the houses are built tight up against the street. Many quaint sights one gets to see here, among which were the barred windows at which young ladies may receive the attention of their lovers, and lovemaking has not gone out of vogue in Mexico to this day.

People live close together here, so a large population gets along here with much smaller territory than the same number of people in the United States. They do not live only along the streets as with us, but they occupy the interior of their city blocks with residences, so that very many more people occupy a block even when the buildings are only one-story structures. So everywhere one went, the thirty thousand inhabitants of the city were everywhere conspicuously in evidence.

Los Animas is located on the northeast corner or side of the city, hugged up to the very confines of the city. San Juan, on the other hand, is located on the southwest corner, also close up to the residences or homes of city dwellers. As we walked on we came to a place where an adobe wall perhaps seven feet high seemed to close off things and we could go no farther. To the right of us I saw a partly collapsed enclosure of what was evidently at one time the garden of a monastery. The only remains of those forgotten days was a figure in stone, perhaps twelve feet high of Christ on the cross standing in the open. All around this statue, the ground was ploughed up and at this very time corn was being planted right to the base of this sacred figure.

Soon we came to a gateway in the wall, and to my surprise my companion turned in here and suddenly I found myself in the country. Before me I saw wheat fields and ploughed fields to the right and to the left of the curving farm road. The grain was in fine condition, turning yellow, and soon ready for the reaper. No house was in sight. San Juan is also a very large farm of over 2000 acres. The land is quite level, not only on this hacienda, but Las Animas as well. In fact the whole Irapuato region, though plateau country, is a great level plain of perhaps ten to fifteen miles in diameter, surrounded by towering mountains, making it an ideal location for human habitation. As we were walking along, admiring the fine fields, arched masonry come into view, stretching far out into the fields. This proved to be the water conveyer for carrying the water for irrigation purposes from the central pumping station of the farm out for distribution into the various parts of the lands. Back of the high masonry, parts of the large buildings could be seen. This estate was kept up in very good condition all through the revolutionary times. The residence on the place is a real mansion of large dimensions, built of large brick. A palisade porch, sixteen feet deep and fifty feet long, faces you as you as you approach the building.

I was asked whether I would like to see their children preparing for children's day exercises on the following day. They took me to large storage building. Behold, in the corner of that building they had improvised a school on the bare ground, with simple seats and desks, and there in this simple way, these intrepid people had gathered their children and were at work training and educating them in the Christian faith and life. About fifty children were there, all of school age, bright, lively intelligent folk, reciting their pieces and singing with vigor, their Christian songs, all of course, in German. Thus early laying such a foundation in the rearing of their youth the perpetuity of their faith and life is assured in their new fatherland.

Under the shade of the large trees in the park, the men, about fifty five in number, seated in a circle, soon asked many questions concerning the great problems of further immigration. They have many friends still in Russia who are not able to finance the trip, so must remain in Russia until, in one way or another, means can be secured to pay for the transportation. After a while, a call was made for services at which they wanted me to preach. This service was held under the great portico, about one hundred and twenty five people being present. These people have not lost their joy for song for a choir of about twenty members sang several fine German chorals. After the service we again sat under the shade trees.

This park would do honor to many a city, yet it is here on a farm. There are magnificent trees, some of them several feet in diameter, flowers, much shrubbery, diagonal and winding paths, a summerhouse, swings and a turning pole. On this farm, the sense for the beautiful need not feel itself neglected, for here nature is given a fine opportunity to set forth her charms and birdlife is here to enrich the enjoyment with song and color. A stroll into the nearby gardens and fields just before sunset reveals a marvelous productivity.

Wheat planted in primitive fashion last November is now on April 12th, just ready for cutting. Alfalfa they cut every thirty days the year round, that is twelve times each year. We walk into and through such a field; the growth is very rank, and excellent hay is fed fresh from the field to the animals. They make no hay for storage. Cantaloupes and watermelons thrive and vegetables are also in good condition. As these Mennonites had bought and moved into this farm in February, they had only been on the farm for about sixty days. The garden had only recently been prepared and sown.

Now peas and beans were just ready for picking. Potatoes were about nine inches tall and lettuce and radishes were being used. Small patches of sweet corn were sending up stalks. The soil is rich and evidently very productive. This farm has been under cultivation for perhaps several hundred years. But no fertilizer seems to be needed to produce good crops. The black loam reaches a depth of about ten feet.

Nightfall prevented further survey of the surroundings, but as in the twilight we strolled toward the house, the tranquility in nature and the balminess of the air made the evening most delightful. One can hardly conceive that they should have such delightful weather the year round, yet this is the claim and they therefore plant and reap in January as well as in June or September. No coal to be brought, no provisions to be made for winter, not even hay to be put up, or any canning to be done from one end of the year to another. One can get fresh vegetables from the garden and some fruit may be gathered at almost any time. Anyone that wishes to do so can go barefooted the year through and always be quite comfortable. Stock needs no special protection, for this is in truth the land of perpetual spring, even though they do have their rainy seasons and their dry seasons.

The pumping of the water on the big farm is done by electricity supplied by the electric works from the city of Irapuato. The big mansion is also lit by electricity. This farm is quite up to date and a pleasant place during the evening. Each of the twenty or more families living in this house occupies separate rooms or spaces. Some day they will convert the patio or inner open court of the house into a chapel. It is large enough to accommodate comfortably a large congregation. What a fine school building that would make when the colony has fully developed and other churches and colonies are also located in that part of Mexico.

The Mennonites in Irapuato are quick to see that it will be well to quickly adapt themselves to the conditions of the country in which they have elected to make their home. They have employed a man from the city who knows both Spanish and German to teach all the people on San Juan Spanish three half days a week. The old people, the young folks and the children receive their instruction in separate classes. The result is that they are acquiring a working knowledge of the Spanish language in a remarkably short time.

These new settlements of the Mennonites in Central Mexico abound in points of interest, and much remains unsaid that would be of interest to many. The writer imagines that he can see these settlements in fifty years from now, as great thriving Mennonite centers, with several active churches of several thousand members each, with many elementary schools for the rearing of the youth in the ways of godliness, a religious school for higher education, a hospital for the care of the sick, and as a center from which will go forth a great missionary activity for the advancement of the Kingdom of our Lord Jesus Christ. But now our journey must be continued, for the objective is to go to Mexico, the national capital.

Unfortunately, the prospects for settlement were not nearly as promising as Mr. Krehbiel's optimistic report suggests.

Here is the formal photo of the group after arrival in Vera Cruz from Russia in October of 1925. My father is on the extreme left in about the 3rd row or fourth row from the rear. Dad's father (with the dark moustache) is the third person from the left holding Aunt Helen on his arm. Uncle Henry Suderman is the first person in the back row on the left side.

Leaving the Ukraine

THE BEST YEARS IN SIBERIA
1912 – 1925, John Peter Suderman

As recorded by my father, in the German language, translated by Elfrieda (Suderman) Block.

I was born on March 15, 1906, in the village of Alexandertahl, in the Ukraine, South Russia in the home of my grandparents, Johann and Aganeta Sudermann.

It is also here that my father, Peter Sudermann, and all his siblings were born and grew to adulthood. My father married Helena Toews in May 1904, and continued to live on his parents' farm for seven more years with his wife. He supervised the farm operations with the assistance of hired Russian workers. I, the first child of my parents and my two brothers, Henry and Leonard were born on this farm. Leonard died a few months after the family left the farm.

I have some fond memories of life on my grandparents' farm. One is the wedding day of my Aunt Agatha and Uncle David Schultz. Another pleasant memory consists of my grandfather taking my brother Henry and me to the store before we left for Siberia. He told us each to choose a hat. He paid for them and we wore them proudly on our way back to the farm and then later as we traveled to our new home.

This picture was taken at the Grandparent's farm in Alexandertahl, Molotschna. My brother Henry and I are sitting in the wagon to the right. We are proudly wearing the hats our grandfather has just purchased.

On June 26, 1912, when I was six years old, my parents and their three young sons left the home of my grandparents to establish their own home in Siberia. Our destination was the newly developing Mennonite settlement in the Slavgorod district.

Our travels by train took us over the Volga River where we crossed a big, newly constructed bridge. This bridge was of special interest to us since we had seen a picture of it in the newspaper. The train crossed the bridge very slowly and we were instructed to stand back from the windows during the crossing.

We traveled to Davlekanovo, near the Ural Mountains where we visited my uncle Jacob Sudermann and his family. Upon leaving those relatives, we again journeyed by rail, crossing the Ural Mountains and into Siberia as far as the city of Omsk. There we boarded a large boat and traveled on the Irtisch River. I could hear the paddles of the paddle wheeler turn and splash the sides of the boat. I believe the paddles were in the centre of the boat. We traveled during the daytime only, so it took 2 1/2 days until we reached Pavlodar. There are my father hired a Kyrgyz person who took us by a large tarantas, one hundred and fifty kilometers to the town of Slavgorod. Some people took us into the village of Schoentahl where we rented rooms from the Friesen family.

In March 1913, my parents purchased property in the village of Gnadenheim, and we moved there a few months later in May. Our new home was a building, which combined the house and barn. It was constructed of clay bricks and had a sod roof. The Russian name for Gnadenheim was one 'Redkaja Dubrovna'. We always called it Gnadenheim although the Postal Service called it 'Redkaja Dubrovna'.

The region where we settled was approximately two hundred and fifty kilometers south of the Trans-Siberian Railway. It was called the Kulunda Steppes, named after the Kulunda River, a tributary of the Ob River. It was also referred to as the Barnaul region after the town of Barnaul, which served as the business center of the surrounding area. Later, the town of Slavgorod was established between the Irtisch and the Ob Rivers to the east. This town became the economic center for the region and the area and was renamed the Slavgorod district.

The Irtisch is the longest river in Russia and the fourth longest river in the world. The Ob and the Irtisch Rivers flow northward and join approximately seven hundred and fifty miles north of Slavgorod. The flat steppes in this region were suitable for agriculture, especially for growing grain. Mennonites established a daughter colony of fifty-five villages in the Slavgorod district. The first settlers arrived in 1908 from South Russia districts such as the Molotschna, the old colony (Chortiza), Sagradovka, Orenburg and Samara.

Many young families and newlyweds with limited financial capital settled in this area. The advantages for them included:

- Cheap fares at one quarter the usual fare, and children, ten and under traveled free.
- Reduced freight rates (1/100 kopek per kilometer per pood (1 pood was approximately forty pounds).
- Land available for a prescribed fee of twenty-five rubles to the settlers with certain tax exemptions for the first five years.
- Military exemption for the first three years.
- An interest free government loan up to one hundred and sixty rubles for establishing settlers.
- Access to crown land forests for firewood and lumber for buildings.
- Credit for the purchase of machinery and seed for up to one hundred and sixty rubles.

The cheap fares and reduced freight rates were a considerable advantage for my parents. We traveled four thousand kilometers, bringing with us a threshing machine, a droschke (four wheeled open carriage), wagon frame and other equipment. I do not know which other benefits my parents utilized, but it appears that they must have taken advantage of some more since I remember hearing discussion regarding them.

Although this area attracted moneyless people, a number of families who sold property in southern Russia came with financial resources. It was easy to identify those who had this advantage. They immediately built good quality homes and had adequate machinery to develop the land compared to those who came without resources and began their new life living in sod huts.

THE INHABITANTS

The Kyrgyz, members of the Mongolian people, were native to this area. They lived on the rolling hills and in valleys where there were pastures and bushes to protect their cattle rather than making their homes on the surrounding flat land as the new settlers did. These native people were nomadic like those in Abraham's day. Their summer homes where mushroom shaped tents that could be set up wherever they found good pasture. In the wintertime when they needed warmer homes, they would move into sod or lime huts. The winters were very cold in Siberia!

The Kyrgyz owned large herds of horses as well as some cattle. They did not cultivate the land for agriculture; rather they used it mostly to water and graze their animals. Their livestock was sheltered under trees. The Kyrgyz always wore heavy clothing. In the summer it protected them from the heat and in the winter, from the cold.

This group of people was Muslims or Mohammedans as we called them. I went through a district where they lived and I observed that when it was time for prayer, they laid out their mats, knelt with their faces to the ground and prayed facing Mecca. The cowherd hired by our village was an old

Kyrgyz man. We had the opportunity to observe him and the ways of his family from time to time.

A large settlement of these people was approximately fifty kilometers north of our settlement. Another one was about 50 km to the south. One day in January, a Kyrgyz man came to buy a horse suitable for pulling a sled. He bought the horses on the condition that in about a month's time when he would be traveling from the settlement north of us to the one south for the total of approximately one hundred kilometers, he would be able to stop over at our place to feed his horses as well as have tea and something to eat.

One day he arrived at our place with three loaded sleds. The group with him was on its way to a wedding. I understood that one of his children was getting married. These people stayed for about two hours. Once inside, they removed their outer clothing revealing their festive attire. The young girls, ten to fourteen years old, had long braids entwined with ribbons from top to bottom with silver pieces in them, each piece about the size of a dime. There were other ornaments on their clothing. I had never before seen people in such fine festive clothes. It was cold and blizzardy outdoors. They put on their warm clothes after they had eaten and their horses had been fed and then set out for the remaining fifty kilometers to the south.

There were Russians in this area besides the native Kyrgyz population. The Russians lived in large villages, usually beside a stream or a tributary like the Kulunda, which flowed into the Ob River. This group of Russians was descendants of prisoners exiled to this region several hundred years before we got there. The Sybarites, as they were referred to, were of noble character. They were fine people who were friendly and hospitable, generally well established and prosperous. We stayed overnight with them from time to time.

A quote from the writings of Gerhardt Fast, "On the Steppes of Siberia" regarding the native population states: surrounding the district of settlements were smaller and larger groups of the native population. East, west and north of the settlements were the descendants of people exiled to this region. Although they spoke Russian, they did not consider themselves to be Russians, rather 'Tschaldony'. I cannot determine the origin of this name nor its' meaning.

This is a peculiar group of people whose lifestyle differs sharply from that of the Russian peasant or the Russian Europeans. Their hospitality, the cleanliness of their homes, their honesty, their dress, especially at their celebrations, indicates that they have a noble and distinguished ancestry. One can assume that their forebears were political prisoners who were exiled to this region. We know that politically suspect people in Russia do not come from the lower classes, rather, mostly from the educated, noble classes. The praiseworthy characteristics of this native group appear to be traces of a decent, superior lineage. These people helped the new settlers overcome the difficulties associated with the early years of settlement by generously contributing toward their daily needs. The settlers received assistance with low-cost agricultural products such as grain, flour, potatoes, meat, eggs, etc. They also received assistance with the sale of horses, cows, pigs, sheep and chickens, thus greatly facilitating the development of the settlement.

It was a pleasure to observe the interaction between the native group and the Mennonites. They quickly established a friendly and growing relationship of trust. It seems as though this group of people was unfamiliar with evil behaviors such as theft, cheating, suspicion and trickery. It was unnecessary to take precautions and lock up or hide personal possessions for safekeeping.

This native group usually lived in very large villages and consequently most of the villagers had their portion of agricultural land a considerable distance from their village. Traveling to and from their property was time consuming so they built primitives shelters, generally earthen huts on their land. They lived in these huts for the entire workweek during the times when the fields required full attention and returned to the village on Sundays. The huts also provided shelter during thunderstorms. Wells provided water for themselves and their animals. These people took provisions along for themselves and their livestock when they worked the fields for extended periods.

Cooking utensils and tools in these huts were accessible for anyone who would occasionally pass through this region. The owner never thought to lock up his equipment since theft was unknown in this culture. It was considered a matter of course that and occasional passing traveler or someone who had lost his way would spend the night and help himself to available food if the owner was absent. This is how the so-called ‘criminal descendants’ behaved.

This group contained many who were exiled for religious reasons, the so-called Starowerzy (Altglaubige). Their remarkable hospitality put some of us to shame. Later, when new settlers arrived from European Russia, especially the Ukraine, and settled in the vicinity of the Siberian inhabitant, this type of hospitality came to an abrupt end because of the rapid changes of land ownership.

VILLAGE LIFE

The region where the Mennonites settled was open, level land, suitable for growing grain. Villages were formed in clusters of two, three or four and stretched over a distance of seventy kilometers. This particular area lay northeast of the town of Slavgorod, which was the business center for the region. The western villages in the vicinity of Slavgorod belonged to the 'Grischshoftka Wollost'. The eastern villages belonged to the 'Orloff Wollost'. Most of the villages consisted of thirty households although some had as few as twenty and some had up to forty, depending on the amount of land being settled. Groups of Lutherans and Catholics also established homes in this vicinity.

Each village had an administrator who was in charge of regulating and administering the village affairs. The concerns of the village were discussed and decided upon at meetings chaired by the 'Schultze'. Included were matters concerning the village herdsman, the common pasture, cultivation of land and regulations regarding new settlers.

The village Schultze and Council hired teachers. Russian government directives regarding the required government school curriculum were sent to the Schultze. Administration of the local Postal Service was also his responsibility.

As soon as the village was organized in the new settlement, poplar and willow saplings were obtained, usually from Samara, and planted in the springtime. Two rows of trees lined the street and eight rows of poplars were at the back of the garden. Two rows of willows separated individual yards. The full-grown trees and hedges prevented snow from piling up in the yard. The settlement had become pleasant and attractive in the years that we lived there as the saplings grew and became tall, stately trees.

A wide street extended through the length of the village. On either side of the street was a four or five foot wide gravel path with a ditch running along side of it. The ditch was approximately one foot deep on one side of the path and about three feet deep on the other side. This enabled the water to drain off into the low-lying wooded area during the spring -thaw or during a rainstorm. We were fortunate that we never experienced a flood during the thirteen years that we live in this village. In the wintertime, five or six foot sunflower stalks were stuck into the snow banks at the side of the road, which joined one village to the next. These markers guided travelers and help them to find their way, especially during a blizzard.

Houses were built in a variety of ways. Sod homes were constructed in the early years, although people with financial means build better quality homes immediately. There were constant improvements as time passed with new homes being built of bricks. Both sod and a brick homes were warm in winter and cool in summer. Sometimes wood was used to build houses but these were just not as warm as the others.

Each village had an elementary school. Usually there was only one teacher who was in charge of sixty students ranging from grades one to six. The school year began in October and lasted through about mid April. Students received Bible instruction in addition to the regular curriculum. This special instruction occurred twice a week, first thing in the morning for both the younger students and the older students.

I was seven years old when I started school in the fall term. Jacob Wedel was my teacher for five years. He was an experienced, successful teacher and well respected in the community. I heard favorable comments about him from time to time as the years passed. Another teacher during that time was your Johann Friesen. Teacher exchanges took place from time to time with four or five fellow teachers participating in order to improve their skills. Their colleagues for purposes of improvement then critiqued their practice lessons.

The Mennonites Brethren congregation, to which we belonged, called their place of worship a 'Versammlungshaus', (a meeting place). The General Conference of Mennonites referred to their place of worship as 'Kirche', and for that reason they were called 'die Kirchliche'. At approximately four or five villages shared a place of worship in a building situated centrally to these villages. We were fortunate to have one in our village.

Church services were conducted every Sunday. An excellent choir sang a number of songs while people were assembling. This was followed by a time of open prayer with a number of lay people participating. The choir then sang another song. A preacher had a short devotional sermon, which was followed by another choir song. Then the main speaker of the morning delivered a sermon and the service was concluded. A visiting preacher, an evangelist, a traveling minister or other special guest sometimes was involved in the service.

Occasionally, a choir conductor's conference was held which featured a trained musician who had been invited to give intensive instruction. This type of conference usually ended with a 'Saengerfest'. The size of the Saengerfest depended on the time of the year and weather conditions.

Winter activities included midweek Bible studies for adults. Sunday school for children was on Sunday afternoon and taught by male teachers. The village teacher was in charge of the Christmas program with all the school children participating. That event was held in the place of worship involving the whole village as long as it was politically possible.

Seeding the land began in the springtime, beginning around the end of April. The five-field system, which was suited for the northern region and had proven itself in Samara, was introduced to our village. This is how it worked:

- The first year, virgin soil was broken by plough and left fallow.
- The second year, wheat was planted after a five-pronged plough turned over the stubble
- The third-year, barley or oats were planted to supply fodder for the horses
- The fourth year, the ground was lightly ploughed and seeded for oats in the springtime. This crop was then harvested in July and ground into fodder for the winter-feeding of cows and horses. Then animals were put on the fields to graze for the remainder of the summer.
- The fifth-year, animals were put in the fields until the end of July when the land was ploughed deeply and planted with rye for the next year.

The entire five years system was repeated on this particular field. This method ensured a maximum return from the land. If the summer was dry, and there was little rain, the harvest was smaller than average. If there was plenty of rain, naturally, the harvest would be a good one. Cattle were driven from one field to another so that the fallow ground could be maintained. The village had about four or five binding machines. The grain was tied into sheaves as long as binder twine was available. It was beautiful to behold sheaves covering the whole field. Most of the farmers used a harvester to push the grain through. This was hard work! The grain was transported home and put into huge piles. Those who owned threshing machines, threshed their grain first, then helped those who had given them assistance, and lastly, help those who did not own machines.

Snow soon covered the countryside with the coming of winter. Cattle remained in the barn where they were fed and cared for. Children returned to school. Winter activities began again in the village, which included regular Bible studies, handwork and woodwork. The cobbler tanned leather and fashioned sandals and soles. However, the blacksmith had more leisure during the wintertime since his busy time had been during the summer months.

Pig butchering was usually done in November. Depending on the size of the family, the number for each household butchered was between two and four pigs. Butchering day he was important and required good organization. The group of people usually four or five couples, was invited by the host family to help with the process. The day's activities began before dawn.

The farmer rose early in the morning to light a fire under the large iron cauldron, which had been filled the previous evening with about forty gallons of water. The pigs were stabbed and scalded in boiling water by eight in the morning. Then they were shaven, hung and eviscerated. The women cleaned the intestines so they could be used for smoked and liver sausage casings. These activities were usually accomplished before all the participants enjoyed the delicious noon meal, prepared by the hostess.

After the noon meal, the carcasses were quartered and spread onto large worktables to be cut into hams, spareribs and other cuts of meat. Headcheese and sausages were prepared. Fat was rendered and cooled to become lard and cracklings.

An early start in the day meant that the pig butchering would be completed in good time for everyone to go to his or her homes for the evening chores. After the regular chores were completed, the participants returned to the home of the hosts and enjoyed a fine supper of fresh liver sausage, spareribs, fruit soup (Obstmus) and hamburgers (Kotletten), - a rich feast indeed!

Pig butchering day was a wonderful occasion for us boys! We came home from school to feast on the different kinds of meat. It also meant that later we had a variety of meats including smoked farmer sausage or liverwurst to take to school with us.

The hams were packed in snow after they had been salted and smoked and kept in the cold granary for the winter. In the summertime, they were kept in the brick stoves packed in ashes were they were well preserved and available as needed. This enabled us to have fresh meats in the summer without the refrigeration we enjoy today.

Often a beef cow was butchered for the winter in addition to the pigs. The meat was cut and packed into a container of snow. Generally, the winter was a more relaxed time after a busy fall.

THE WAR YEARS -- WORLD WAR ONE

My father was conscripted into service by the Russian government as soon as World War one broke out in September 1914. He was assigned to work in the forest (alternative service) near the city of Tomsk. A huge forest called Taiga was near the river and the town of Taiga. The forest was extraordinarily big and dense with the evergreen trees growing to a height of one hundred and fifty feet and the birch trees to a height of one hundred feet. The trunks were mostly bare with branches at the top of the trees. Only birch trees were cut for firewood and hauled to Tomsk.

I had to help with much of the work on our farm when my father was away from home. In the second year of the war, a refugee family with seven children from Wolimen, Poland, became the responsibility of the village of Gnadenheim. My mother decided, with my father's approval, to take this family, whose name was Nachtigal, into our home so that we could have assistance with a household, the cattle and all the other work.

My mother took us, that is, my baby brother Jacob, Henry and me to Taiga near Tomsk where Papa was felling trees. The trip covered a distance of seven hundred kilometers – two hundred and fifty kilometers by sled to Tatarskaja and the remainder of the journey by train. Everything I saw on this trip was fascinating for me as it would be for any ten year old - especially the amazing forest with apparently five varieties of coniferous trees and the birch trees reaching a height of one hundred feet.

The cleared area got bigger, steadily moving the men farther away from their home base. Consequently, some of the men moved out of the barracks, rented a complex of houses from a Russian and lived there in order to be nearer to their work-place. A number of these men sent for their wives so that the families could be together. A group of like-minded people conducted church services in the building, which housed the kitchen and dining hall. A Mr. Bergen, who was part of this group, was a trained teacher and taught four students, which included two girls from a Loewen family, my brother Henry and me for two evenings each week.

We lived in a blockhouse, which contained a number of empty beehives. Papa built a wooden barrier along one wall and a wooden platform against it to serve as beds for all the family. In the middle of our space was a wood stove which was stuffed with blocks of birch wood so that we had a warm place. The stove was also used for cooking. Our bread was obtained from the main camp kitchen. Henry and I had to get milk from the landlord of the housing complex who owned a herd of 20 to 25 milk-producing cows.

Near the blockhouse was a large barrack housing Austrian prisoners of war. They baked wonderful rye bread so that Henry and I went there from time to time to buy a freshly baked loaf of rye bread. We had to pass by a little sod hut built partly into a hill. There was always someone who had trespassed the rules in some way and had to spend a few days as punishment in this place. Sometimes we would stand by the door and quietly listen to them. We felt sorry for these people. These Austrian prisoners also felled trees for the government.

And that is how we spent a most interesting winter. In March my father hired someone to cut his quota of wood so he could return home with us for a period of time. We journeyed by train as far as Tatarskaja , then the remaining two hundred and fifty kilometers to our settlement by state post. The distance between post houses was usually about forty to fifty kilometers. We traveled in two horse-drawn sleighs because the roads were covered with snow at this time of the year.

The coachman and my parents with my little brother, Jacob, were in the first sleigh. My brother, Henry and I were in the second sleigh with all the families' baggage. We were tucked in with heavy for blankets so that only the side view was visible. A line attached to the horse pulling our sleigh was laid beside us and was available in we needed to guide the horse. However, this proved to be unnecessary since the horse was well trained and followed the first sleigh without any assistance. I gave a tug once and the horse sped up so that it almost crashed into the first sleigh. Needless to say, I didn't pull the line again.

We traveled day and night. Everything was ready and waiting for us when we arrived at a post house. The Siberian term for that type of post is in 'Jamschtschima'. We would go into the building and quickly eat and drink hot tea from a samovar while the horses were exchanged. Then, after half an hour, we were off again! In that way the trip went smoothly and quickly until we arrived close to our settlement.

The summer of 1916 was quite dry and windy and our crop was poor. It was often difficult to get the help we needed so that we had to frequently manage on our own as best we could. I was drawn into helping with farm chores more often than I had been previously. In the winter I had to help with the chores in addition to going to school.

In March 1917, the pictures of the Czar and Czarina were removed from the wall of the school. We were told that the Czar had abdicated the throne and was no longer in power. People became anxious and apprehensive about the future. The first socialist government was now in charge and lasted until the October Revolution when the Communists took power in St. Petersburg.

In 1915, Papa received permission to come home for four weeks during threshing time. Then in 1917, he was able to come home for fifty days and was able to accomplish the seeding of our fields with the help of Henry and myself. My brother and I had to help a lot during the whole summer. Papa then came home for good in December of that year. He had served the government for three years and three months. Normality returned to our home with my father's return.

The next two years were very interesting. Siberia had become independent. Admiral Koltshak settled in Omsk with a large group of military men. They were part of the White Army and had an alliance with England and France as well as trade contracts with the United States. Ships traveled back and forth along the Kurdish River to the Polar Sea. Military uniforms, ammunition, rifles, cannons and large military trucks were imported to Siberia from England. The ships were then loaded with wheat for their return to England.

Soldiers occupied the marketplace in Slavgorod. They practiced their drills, marching back and forth. It was most fascinating for me to see military men march during the summer months and big trucks drive back and forth. The local economy thrived in 1918 as a result of the brisk trade with other countries. Wheat prices were exceptionally good so that my parents acquired machinery such as a binder and other necessary farm equipment. The economic upswing of 1918 – 1919 was evident throughout the district.

Times changed when the Communists took charge of Omsk in late fall of 1919. The whole winter was a very depressing one for the farmers because they had to concern themselves with the supply of grain. Communists from European Russia traveled along the Trans-Siberian Railway and stopped just short of the city of Omsk where they spent time preparing for a takeover. They were ready by late November when it turned cold after a mild fall.

One day everything broke loose! At five o'clock in the morning, a large group of horseback riders entered the city of Omsk. They took over important places and achieved occupation of the prison by shooting from the high church tower, thereby forcing the prison gates to open. Other riders demanded entry into the hospital. Fighting between the Communists and the White Army began during the day. The Communists quickly gained the upper hand in spite of their opponent's considerable military strength. The White Army was defeated mainly through the traitorous acts of sabotage by some of its own soldiers. These men had engaged in actions such as pouring water into the gas tanks of their own trucks the previous night. Thousands of defeated soldiers were forced to flee eastward on foot. Some of the soldiers were able to escape by train. However, train travel was very irregular during this time so that great numbers of soldiers perished. Many froze to death during their flight, especially in December when the weather became bitterly cold. Some found refuge in empty railcars, but many became ill and died.

Omsk became a place of great sadness! The Communists assumed power. Thousands of people died as a result of the typhus epidemic or by freezing to death. My brother-in-law, who witnessed some of these events, told me some horrific stories regarding this time.

Returning to my school days, plans and preparations were made to establish a high school in our village for the fall of 1919. I had just completed six years at the village elementary school. After seeding time was completed, a date was scheduled to examine students for acceptance into high school. Our teachers spend additional time for a week reviewing subject matter with the eligible students to prepare us for the entry examinations. Five students from our village were candidates for these exams. Students from a number of other villages came as well. There were five students from the village of Orloff who kept telling us how advanced they were in mathematics and seemed convinced that none of the rest of us were as skilled as they were. When the results of the math exam were given, we discovered that our group had obtained the highest marks. I found the math exam to be quite easy. Our group of five students was the first to complete the exams and achieved the highest marks in every subject, which pleased our teacher very much.

Classes began in the fall and were held in our church building, which had been divided into two classrooms. One teacher was Heinrich Willms who taught German and religion. The other was Olga Poledimova, a fine Russian woman who had fled St. Petersburg with her mother. Her father, who had been in charge of the Czar's horses, was a victim of the revolution. The Czar's mother, the dowager Czarina, had attended Olga's high school graduation banquet. I liked Olga's method of teaching. She was a good communicator – her lessons in world history, geography and Russian language were clear and interesting. They awakened and stimulated my curiosity to see more of the world. Olga was a member of the Baptist denomination but frequently attended the services in our church.

The school expanded to three classrooms the following year. Olga's sister, Eugenia, was hired as the third teacher. She did not teach with the same clarity and interest as her sister did. She taught us a literary play called in 'Revisor' as well as other pieces. These were performed at two places and were well received. All that took us on a field trip to a Russian village called Tlinku, which was sixty kilometers away, near the Kulunda River. We were billeted at a large school. The weather was warm so we played in the water during the day. The women teachers accompanied the students and organized everything with the Russians, which included having a meal together. I came home exhausted from that trip, went straight to bed and fell asleep immediately. I had forgotten quite a lot of the details about the outing, but I remember having a very good time!

School changed considerably for the next year. One of the teachers, Mr. Willms, died as a result of typhus and Olga Poledimova left to continue her studies in medicine, later practicing as a medical doctor in southeast Siberia. Three new teachers came to teach. They were all from the same family, father, son and daughter whose surname was Modin. I began the school year but was forced to quit. The operation of the school could not continue because the settlement, unable to deliver the grain for sale, could not support the teachers.

The following year the government made an offer to those who had already begun high school training to continue their education in Slavgorod, free of charge. Board and room could be obtained at a very reasonable rate. I was one of five Mennonite youth who spent a year attending the Russian state high school. We shared boarding facilities with Russian students. The Moldins (father, son, and daughter), who had been teaching in the high school in Gnadenheim, lived in the opposite end of the same boarding house. All three were very were highly educated individuals. The elder Modin was a former professor. I spent the school year having new experiences but unfortunately I did not learn a great deal. I certainly did not want to become a teacher!

I stayed at home the next year and tried my hand at farming. My brother Henry, and I experimented with a number of things on the farm. One thing we tried during the winter was to train a pair of horses to go in tandem. We had a fine team and traveled around with it, at times with considerable speed.

The next year there was an announcement that the Bible school in Davelkanovo would operate for the second year. The school was situated in European Russia, two thousand kilometers by train from our home.

I had a strong desire to attend this school. My parents consented to my wish so I left in the fall of that year for studies at Bible School called 'Licht im Osten", (Eastern Light). I lived with my uncle Jacob Sudermann's family. There were only six students attending the school, two from Alma

Ata, two or three from Omsk, one local person and myself from the Slavgorod district. We had an excellent instructor whose name was Karl Friedricksen. This individual had studied at St. Chrischona, Basel, Switzerland. He was very knowledgeable in terms of the Bible and gave me a solid biblical foundation, which helped me spiritually as the years went by.

I never became a minister but Bible school training gave me a basis for making decisions in every day practical situations and discerning God's will during the course of my life. I am grateful to God for this experience and I have never regretted spending a year in Bible school.

INDUSTRY

Industry in the Slavgorod district was underdeveloped and deficient. There were beginnings of some industrial endeavors, which could not continue to develop when the Communists took over the government.

The Danish Butter Export Association had a number of branches in Siberia, which included one in Slavgorod. I do not know exact date how the company operated in this area or about all of its productions. However, I do know that they produce the highest quality of butter. The company established butter factory in Gnadenheim in the year 1923 to 24 and brought the necessary equipment such as special packing barrels, and a huge cream separator and a large butter churn that was run by actual horsepower.

Farmers brought their fresh milk on a daily basis, which was then weighed and put through the cream separator. Skim milk could be taken home again and used however one wanted to use it. The cream was retained by the factory and made into quality sweet butter the same day. It was then transported to Slavgorod once a week and put into warehouses. Butter was exported in special containers and its quality was carefully monitored. Whenever the butter was not up to top quality, everything was immediately examined and corrected.

The dairy was a great economic boost to our village and provided good monthly cash income for the farmers. A farmer who own five or six cows could earn about thirty rubles per month from the dairy alone. The dairy operated very well and continued on after the revolution. The Danish Butter Association had been in Siberia since about 1900 with dairies in a number of districts. These dairies where the main source of income for the region of Omsk and for farmers along the railway track before the grain export existed.

The wheat export developed during the Japanese war in 1904. It became the main industry for the whole district after that point and continued to be that as long as we lived there.

Another thriving industry important to our area where flour mills. No large mills existed in Siberia when the Mennonites arrived. However, approximately a dozen mills were built within about five years of their arrival. Small ones could be found here and there throughout the district. A large mill, one of the best, was the Tjart mail in Halbstadt, approximately seven kilometers from our village. This mill was built in 1911 to 1912 for 135,000 rubles. It was equipped with new machines imported from Germany. It had a capacity to mill 2500 pood (over 90,000 pounds) of wheat in twenty-four hours into a superior quality of flour.

People came here to have their wheat milled from within a radius of one hundred kilometers. I personally went to this mill to deliver wheat. I received a certain amount of flour and bran in return. The communists expropriated this mill in 1922-23, but then it slowly deteriorated until it was finally totally ruined. This happened to the other flourmills as well.

Some Friesen brothers built another large mill in Slavgorod. These men went to purchase machines for the mill. However, when they returned from the trip, they became ill and died as a result of typhus so that the mill was never completed and operational.

The tannery was another industry in our area. We would take good quality hides to the tanner so leather could be prepared to make soles, halters and lines. The leather craftsman in our village was highly skilled and made fine saddles and other leather items.

A blacksmith was required to sharpen ploughs and repair machines. However, during wartime, I had to ride to Liebentahl in order to service our ploughshares there. This village was approximately three kilometers from our place and was inhabited by German Catholics. We had our own village blacksmith again when the war ended and the men returned home.

About three wood craftsmen in our village fashioned simple furniture, doors, windows, and doorframes and other wood products.

It was a great treat for us boys when our father took us to Slavgorod to purchase supplies for the winter. We went to the department store by the marketplace in the city. I especially enjoyed buying warm felt boots. There was a great selection of footwear from which we could choose in order to get exactly what we wanted. I was always amazed by the immense selection of goods whenever I entered the store.

I was especially impressed with the large modern, silver-white 'National' cash register. A smart looking woman (cashier) sat at the cash register and handled the money. This was probably the only machine of its kind I saw there.

This store called 'Winokurov' was in Slavgorod when we first moved to Siberia. However, it shut down when supplies were not available in 1916-17. The proprietor of this store owned another store in Kamen on the Ob River, which was actually his main store. We went there once to purchase some paint.

Smaller business establishments included a dry goods store (cloth and sewing notions), a bookstore, plus a firm that sold farm implements and parts for machinery.

The village of Gnadenheim was keen about cultivating good stock so a stallion was imported from Germany. The stallion was an'Oldenburger' breed, similar to what Canadians call a 'Belgian' horse. The descendants of this stallion were superior horses, bigger than the Siberian horse and very handsome. We worked this kind of horse for three or four years, traded it with another village, and had it returned to us after four years.

A purebred shorthorn bull was imported from England, which was good for milk production. Excellent results were obtained when the shorthorn was crossed with the red German cow. There was a good market for these outstanding cattle. Russians came from far and wide to observe and check them out. They would reserve the calf whenever they observed a pregnant milk cow. A bull-calf fetched an especially good price.

Many farmers raised sheep for wool. The sheep were shorn and the wool was spun in the winter months. Many spinning wheels were acquired, some of which were manufactured locally. Consequently, we had warm stockings and mittens during the turbulent years when those items were unavailable in the stores.

GRAIN SUPPLY AND DELIVERY

The railway was extended to Slavgorod in the summer of 1916, forty kilometers from where we lived. All our grain was delivered to Slavgorod so that it could be shipped by rail. A large group consisting of ten to twenty people from our village traveled together forming a caravan with their horse-drawn wagons filled with grain so that they could arrive safely at the required time.

The wagons were unloaded beginning with the first wagon in the line to the last one. Some men stood on the top of the sacks of grain so that they could pick up the sacks and lay them on the shoulders of the men who carried them to the granary. When the granary was filled to a certain point, sacks were then carried up stairs and emptied form the top until the granary was full. Emptied wagons were parked and guarded, usually by a person who had difficulty with the physical exertion required for handling the heavy sacks. In that way, the whole operation was organized in an efficient way. The farmers then spent the night in the town and returned home the next day. The trip was a pleasant experience in the summer time, less pleasant during inclement weather.

DIFFICULTIES DURING THIS PERIOD OF HISTORY

In 1920, all grain had to be delivered to Slavgorod. The following year, in 1921, warehouses for grain were established in the settlement. I was fifteen years old and still going to school at the time so I was able to make observations about the things that were happening. I will relate what I am able to recall from that period.

Inspectors were ordered to come to the villages and had the authority to arrest and jail anyone who delivered less grain than they judged to be sufficient. They arrested two men from each village and had them incarcerated as a warning to others. These prisoners often contracted typhus and died. The situation often became critical for many farmers in the villages because it was difficult to get everything done promptly in the wintertime and in addition, some people had no grain left.

Warehouses for grain were built outside the settlements after the following Christmas. A warehouse was built by the owners of Marten's flourmill in Alexandrovka and one by the owners of the Tjart flourmill in Halbstadt. Mr. Dyck in Orloff owned a large barn (Scheune), which was used for this purpose as well. This is how the winter passed. Additional problems arose because some of the storage places were not waterproof so that the grain spoiled when the thaw came in the springtime. Many farmers did not have wheat seed or feed for their animals. Flour also became scarce as time passed.

What was to be done? Some farmers helped themselves to the grain that was stored in the warehouse, taking it back for seed and feed for the animals as well as some for flour.

Several farmers even got some grain to sell. Mr. Martens, the miller, who stored a lot of wheat, assisted quite a few of them to obtain grain for their requirements by making a deal, stipulating that they would repay him double the amount after they had harvested the crops.

It was possible to be deceptive about the grain delivery at certain storage places, especially in Slavgorod where all the granaries were located. A farmer might take a few fine large hams to the person who operated the scales, who in return wrote receipts for an additional hundred pood of grain so that the farmer would get credit for more grain than he actually delivered. The comments I make come from personal observation.

My parents did not conduct business like that. Instead, they were always compliant with the demands and totally honest about their deliveries. They seeded two properties because our neighbor, J Friesen, needed assistance. He was a teacher who had two crippled children. My parents always gave him half of the crop. We were able to make adequate deliveries of grain because we had good crops during those years.

Grain had to be delivered to Slavgorod in summertime so it could be loaded on to the train. There were many shortages in the amounts delivered so the government commissioned an investigation. However, this investigation could not proceed because a fire destroyed the books and records regarding the deliveries from the district of Slavgorod.

A number of men were arrested following the fire and put into jail. Among them was Mr. Martens, the mill owner from Alexandrovka who had a large wheat storage building and had assisted many of the farmers with seed grain.

I attended the state high school in Slavgorod in the year 1922-23 together with some other Mennonite youth. This was a boarding school with the living facilities across the street. One bright morning in March, we met soldiers on the street who were escorting a group of thirteen prisoners. Each prisoner wore a heavy chain, which was attached to his left hand and his left foot. The prisoners were forced to walk wearing these chains. I was horrified at this sight! I had never seen anything like this before. The accused were taken from the jail to the sports field, which we had occasionally used for practices but now used as a courtroom facility. After school, we would go to observe the proceedings since they were held in this open space.

The thirteen men were accused of irregularities and of falsifying information regarding the deliveries of grain. I observed a trial that lasted three or four days. Mr. Martens, the mill owner was being interrogated one day while I was there to watch the proceedings. He was sitting in the defendant's seat with his defense counsel. He faced intense cross-examination but maintained that he had simply helped the farmers.

The judges were seated in front of a table that was covered with a red cloth with a hammer and sickle emblazoned on the centre of it. The complainant was sitting at one end of the table. I had a negative impression of this man and his accusatory remarks affected me deeply. I was horrified when at one point; he spoke for about one hour, making strong charges against Mr. Martens. I hoped I would never ever have to be in this type of court situation.

My heart ached for Mr. Martens. He lived approximately ten kilometers from where we lived. His mill had been built about three or four years previous to this time. We never used his mill since our grain had been taken to the Tjart mill, which milled a better grade of flour and was about seven kilometers from our place.

Mr. Martens, the only Mennonite in this group of thirteen prisoners, always answered very calmly and insisted that he had only helped the farmers. The farmers generally testified favorably on his behalf. However, the plaintiff continued with his harsh words.

Finally, the judge, who sat in the centre, gave the sentences. The head manager of the main grain delivery warehouse and Mr. Martens were sentenced to death and were taken to Omsk where they were shot in the summertime. The other prisoners received sentences of fifteen, ten and five years. Two prisoners were acquitted. I remember the trial with considerable fear and consternation, thinking that I would never want to experience something like that myself.

THE SUMMER OF 1922

The summer of 1922 was somewhat unusual because of the famine in European Russia. Many people came from those regions, some who brought articles such as clothing, bicycles and a variety of other things to sell or trade. The government had apparently given them special transport and freight opportunities. We went to Halbstadt with a load of wheat to have it milled at the flourmill and traded our flour for a selection of European goods.

We had completed the seeding and were not particularly busy at this point but my father hired a man who had come from his home in the Ural Mountains where he was an iron smelter. This man was short, broad and strong, about thirty-five years old. I observed him from time to time, because he seemed somewhat unusual. His behavior was exemplary, never disagreeable or underhanded. He was quiet, but friendly, dependable and diligent. I asked Papa about him. My father replied that the man had a wife and two children who were going hungry.

I was never aware of any discord or any problem between Papa and him. This man always stayed at home and never spent any money, saving everything he earned. I do not know if he smoked. When harvesting was over, we gave him his payment of wheat for which he was very grateful. My father and I drove him to the train station and helped him load his grain on to the train. The government did not charge a fee to ship the wheat since it was for his family's personal use. I do not know if he was able to travel free of charge. I was often moved and very impressed when I thought about his conduct.

THE END OF LIFE IN RUSSIA FOR US

In 1919-20, a group of three men were appointed to a commission for the purpose of going to America via the Black Sea and Constantinople, Turkey. This commission from the Molotschna Colony consisting of Benjamin Unruh, Abram Friesen and Mr. Warkentin, was to investigate the feasibility of the Russian Mennonites immigrating to the United States or Canada. The United States was not open to immigrants but Canada was willing to receive them.

The commission began negotiations and preparations for immigration. Reports concerning these negotiations were sent to the various districts in Russia where the Mennonites lived. We were made aware of the proceedings and followed the reports with great interest. Immigration fever grew in the colonies as a result.

Canada and Russia signed an agreement which guaranteed thousands permission to leave Russia and immigrate to Canada. In 1923, a group of Mennonites from South Russia, consisting of mainly former refugees who had lost everything during the revolution, left the country for Canada. More people left in 1924. Many of these were from South Russia with the addition of some from the northern districts of Russia.

A larger quota was negotiated for 1925, so our family decided to leave Russia as well. That year, on the first day of August, our family was part of a group of twelve families that left Slavgorod. Our family did not require credit for traveling since we were able to finance our trip ourselves.

The next year, in 1926, four hundred people left Slavgorod, financed by credit, and arrived in Quebec on November 25h. These people were divided into groups and taken to Manitoba, Saskatchewan, and Alberta to make their new homes in the new country.

After Stalin came to power in Russia in the following year, it became very difficult to emigrate. Small groups were able to leave in 1928 and in 1929. In 1929-1930, Mennonites by the thousands fled to Moscow (estimated to be about 30,000) where several trains were filled with the fortunate ones who then left the country. Emigration was halted at that point and the rest of the Mennonites were sent back to their homes. No Mennonites were allowed to leave after that.

Dortmund and Beyond

Uncle Victor Suderman discovered a dissertation published by Bruno Meyer at the Philipps University in Marburg, Germany in 1930. This dissertation, in the German language, documents the story of the Sudermann family in northern Europe and their contributions from the early thirteenth Century to the seventeenth Century. The foreword details the rise and fall of their activity in the trade and organization of the German Hanse as part of the Hanseatic League. The thesis suggests that the rise and fall of the German Trade Hanse was very much aligned to the energetic participation of this particular family. The family, referred to as an old, patrician, trade family, the Sudermanns, was located in the significant trade City of Dortmund.

Credit is given for the sources for the material in Bruno Meyer's dissertation. These sources were found in the Publications of the Historical Society of the Hanse, The Historical Society of Dortmund and the History of the County of Mark as well as the Public Records Office in London and the Archives in Krakau. He was able to obtain the genealogical material from handwritten records in the Dortmund Archives.

His additional sources were in the books and writings of many other authors such as Dietrich Shafer, E. Daenell, J Hansen, R. Hapke and others. He cites many other sources for information on the land holdings, tax payments and local customs and circumstances.

Credit is also given to L. V. Winterfelds in the Dortmund Archive for providing a relatively comprehensive genealogical table of the Sudermann family.

My belief that this family is probably the family of origin of the Sudermanns that live in Canada and the USA today is the fact that I recall my father saying that the oral history of the Sudermann family of which he was a part, was that it had originated in Dortmund. This is oral history and we have no written verification to make the connection from the seventeenth Century to the exodus from Poland by the Sudermanns to the Ukraine in the eighteenth Century. Hopefully, the future may yet yield more information in this area. The various migrations from the Ukraine, starting in 1874 and later in the 1920's brought most of the Sudermanns to America from the Ukraine. Many of those who remained, have in the 1990's and 2000's moved to Germany.

The dissertation gives an overview of the Sudermann's prominence and activity in Dortmund and the family's spread to the neighboring cities of Soest and Cologne. Because of their very active trade engagement, they also established families in Krakau as well as other northern European cities such as Bruges, Antwerp, London and the Baltic centers, such as Bergen.

As early as the first half of the 13th Century, the name of Sudermann was on Dortmund records. The first Sudermann named Walbert Sudermann (I, 1) a city council member appears on records in 1230. The records show Engelbert Sudermann (I, 2) as Council member in 1239 who is still shown as a member as late as 1255. Of the same generation is Johann Sudermann (I, 3), a judge. There is no information to show the relationship between these three men.

The next, the second generation of Sudermanns includes three brothers, Bertram (I, 4), Johann (I,5) and Hildebrand (I,6). Of these three, Bertram and Hildebrand are also on record as Council members. Bertram's sons (III, 4), Heinrich, Bertram, Arnold, Hildebrand, and Johann were exceptionally active administratively and financially. Johann and Hildebrand were businessmen. They were particularly active in trade with the Flemish and English import and export trade. Heinrich and Bertram were educated in Bologna and had careers in the church. Heinrich had a brilliant career as a resident Curial, a member of the Papal court. Bertram began as a local priest in the main cathedral of Dortmund, St. Reinoldi but returned to public service for the city. Arnold remained active in city administration where he served as city council member and then as Burgomaster from 1340 to 1357.

The third generation was particularly prominent in its activities and contribution to the City of Dortmund. They spawned an extraordinarily large family with a wide variety of occupations and family interests that ranged from business, politics to the church.

In the fourth generation, Arnold (IV, 48), son of Arnold occupies the most outstanding significance. For most of his life, he was occupied in the service of the city, which spanned the years, 1378 to 1433. Apparently, the years, 1388 to 1389 were particularly challenging financially and he faced the problems of making significant decisions affecting the prosperity or distress of the city.

In the same generation, Johann (V, 58), son of Johann, became a very prominent businessperson. Many who were not active in business and trade pursuits became very active as city officials and clergy. Records show that there were considerable illegitimate children who were also provided with a modest livelihood by those in administrative positions.

During the fifth generation, movement to other nearby cities and centers became evident. Particularly to Soest where records show they amassed huge land acquisitions. Christine (IV, 50), the sister of Arnold moved to Soest in 1340 and Arnold, mayor of Cologne, also moved there in 1378. A Sifrid Sudermann came to Soest in 1355 and a Detmar Suderman in 1356. Johann Suderman, who had lived in Bruges, came to Soest in 1342. There was a strong trade connection between Soest and Dortmund. A financial collapse in 1400 in Dortmund resulted in movement to and the strengthening of trade with the City of Cologne. At that point we see a strong movement of family members to Cologne.

Already in the first half of the 13th Century, a significant move was made by a part of the Sudermann family from Dortmund to the city of Krakau in Poland. Records show that Heinrich Sudermann was "Ratsherr" in Krakau in 1302, 1309 and in 1312. Also prominent in the next generation were his sons Hanko and Heinko.

The dissertation makes a strong argument that the Sudermann family took a strong position in respect to power and governance in the city of Dortmund. It aligned itself with the traditional and powerful families in Dortmund and protected the positions of power from influence of the 'nouveau riche'. Further, it gave little assistance to the ambitions, complaints and desires of the ordinary citizens. This was evidenced by the conflict that erupted over the use of common grazing rights, land cultivation rights as well as herdsman rights in 1340 to 1347. The outcome gave rights to the citizens even though the Sudermanns claimed traditional private ownership and were supported by the Count of the district of Mark against the citizenry.

Another issue arose that challenged the traditional right of the patrician families to dominate the council and mayoralty positions given to them as privileges by decree of the Kaiser in 1332. The political privileges were also imbedded in the Reingoldigilde, a particular trade guild, which they were also forced to give up. The family, nonetheless, attempted to regain these privileges.

These are the genealogical charts set out in the thesis.

STAMMTAFEL DER FAMILIE SUDERMANN.

Die genealogische Stammfolge wurde von L. von Winterfeld auf Grund Dortmunder, Soester und Kölner Unterlagen aufgestellt (s. Dortmunder Stadtarchiv, Abteilung Patriziat, Mappe Sudermann). Ich habe die Krakauer Linie neu hinzugefügt und die genealogisch nicht anschließbaren Sudermanns in die mutmaßliche Generationsfolge eingereiht.

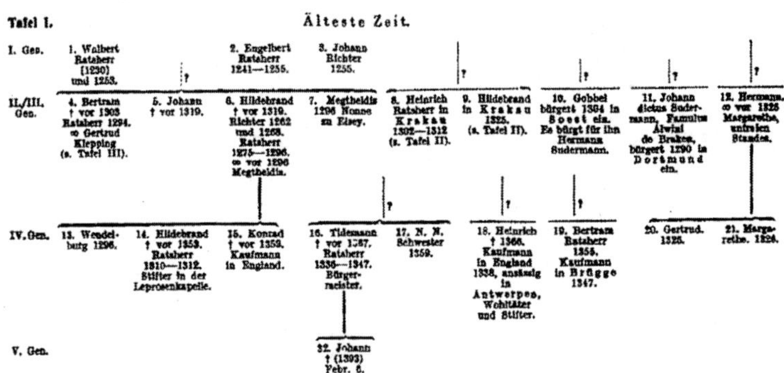

Table 1

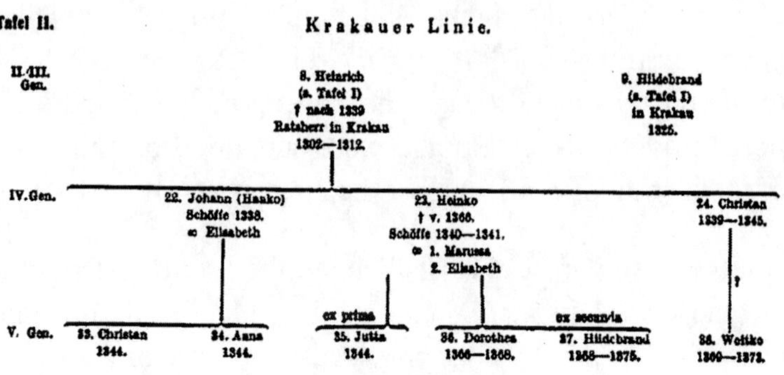

Table 2

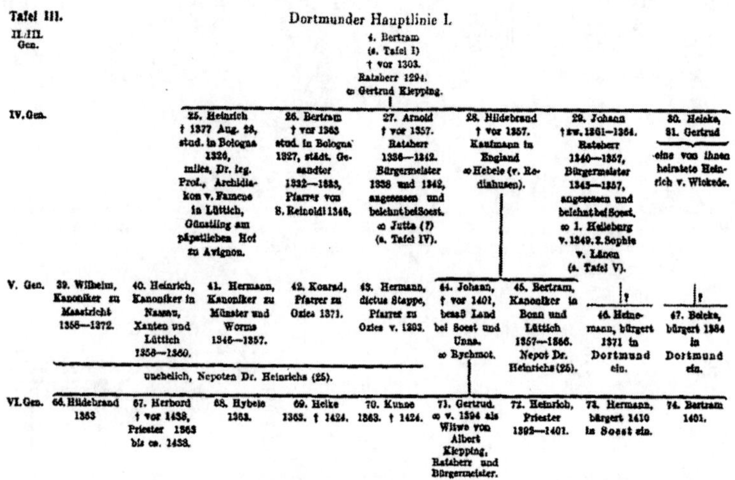

Table 3

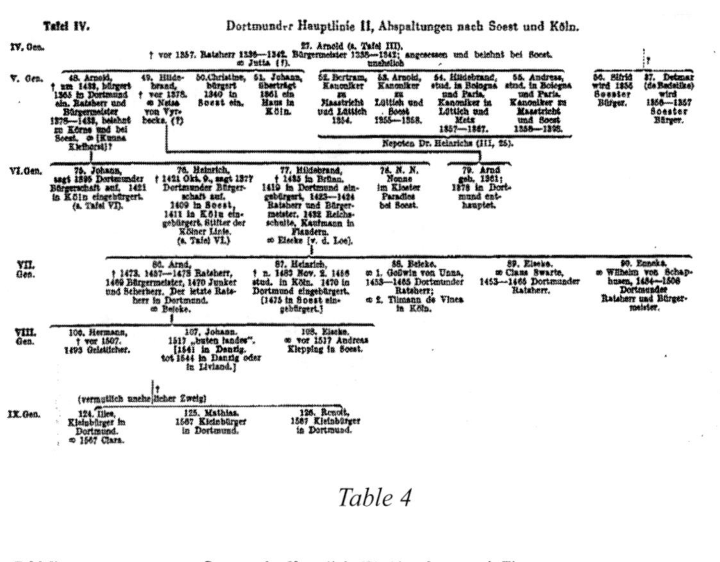

Table 4

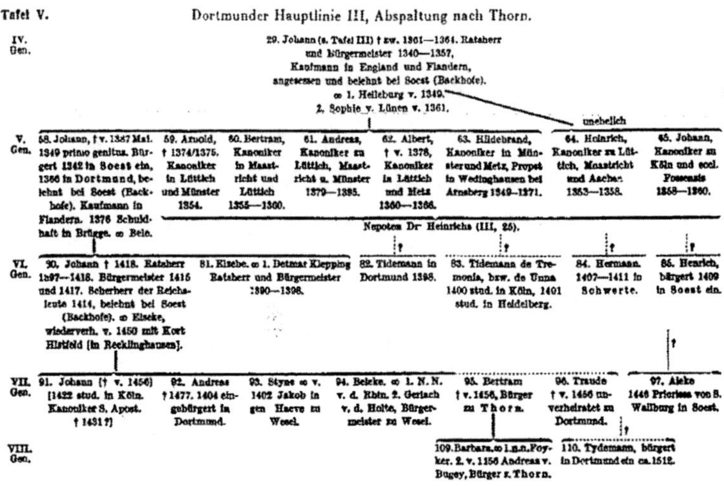

Table 5

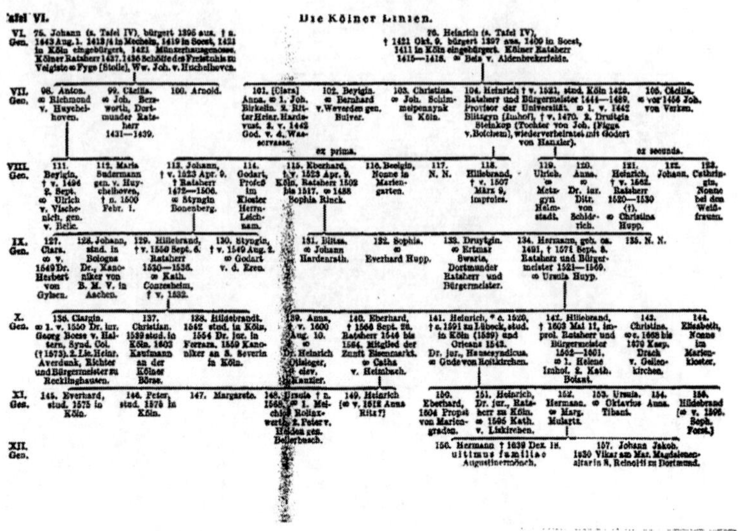

Table 6

In 1346, Bertram Sudermann, the parish priest to St. Reinoldi, with priests from neighboring parishes formed a 'brotherhood' that took over the task of choosing the council members until the year 1400. At that point, the strength of the citizens who had risen to prominence, but were not long standing patrician families, asserted their rights. Finally after many adverse attempts they eventually gained such rights in 1400.

The participation of the Sudermann family was also strong in respect to the political problems of that era. An example is the issue of the Dominican Monk's struggle to establish a presence in Dortmund between 1319 and 1332. The city council opposed their application and the names of the priest, Bertram Sudermann (III.26) and the council member, Hildebrand Sudermann (I.14) feature prominently among those opposed to what were considered a "beggar" order. The Dominicans registered a complaint with Court in Cologne in 1324. The Archbishop of Cologne as well as the King of Bohemia supported the application of the Dominicans but they were unable to persuade the city of Dortmund to change its position. The officials in Cologne declared a church ban against the city that was then appealed to the Pope, resident in the City of Avignon in France. A counter appeal was launched by the city of Dortmund and Heinrich Sudermann (III, 25) was sent as the attorney to argue the case for Dortmund. After delays and a long period of argument the case was finally determined in support of the Dominican Order in 1332.

In coming into conflict with the Archbishop of Cologne and the Pope in Avignon they had gained the support of King Ludwig of Bavaria who supported the Franciscan Order. The town council proceeded to send a delegation, which included Bertram Sudermann in 1332 to King Charles in Nuremburg. They were able to achieve a very satisfactory outcome documented in the famous painting, 'Goldenen Bulle' on August 25, 1332 which includes the delegation of Bertram Sudermann, clericus civitatis, and Hermannus Clepping, civis, in the picture. The privileges that had existed for the patrician families were confirmed by royal decree. This Bertram Sudermann is also a representative of the German Hanse in Bruges in 1347.

The dissertation further documents the frequent participation of various family members in the political wars that were often related to trade issues and competition with such regional towns as Muenster and Luebeck. It documents the payment of ransom money for release of captives, of diplomatic engagement, the signing of peace treaties and highlights the competence of various members as knights. In the area of the church, major conflicts required repeated delegations between Archbishops and the Pope to regulate areas of influence and control. The ban would often be imposed by authorities and then rescinded after negotiations.

Frequently, the City of Dortmund found itself in conflict. If it supported the position of the Pope in Avignon and the City of Cologne, it would find itself in conflict with King Ludwig of Bavaria and the Pope in Rome. It was a time of Knighthood and loyalty and support were constantly in negotiation. Johann Sudermann (III, 29) of this generation, was very active as Master of the Knights and was himself captured and ultimately redeemed for a large ransom.

Active trade resulted in the ability to acquire riches and property. Records show the payment of huge sums to support knights in armor. Various family members are shown to have lent large sums of money to the King of England and given security in huge sums to the City of Dortmund as a result of debts accumulated during feuds and wars. Hildebrand Sudermann was the representative that spent time in London facilitating trade and the lending of money. The Sudermann property holdings encompassed villages, forest tracts, pasture and farmlands as well as significant properties and estates in and around Dortmund, and Soest. Dozens of villages are listed as having significant Sudermann land interests.

The endowments in the many churches and cloisters of Dortmund reflect their wealth as well as their interest in the church. The most significant church in Dortmund was the Reinoldikirche, which was richly endowed by Dr. Heinrich Sudermann. This was the same Heinrich that was sent to the Pope in Avignon to negotiate the Dominican issue. His father Bertram and Uncle Johann endowed the building of the Peter and Paul altar in the same church. Johann and Hildebrand endowed an altar in the Nikolaikirche. Hildebrand donated a large property to the Johanniskapelle in order to support a leper colony and to pay for a rector on an endowed basis. Many other specific gifts are documented. Interestingly, a goodly number of endowments were for the purpose of saying daily prayers for deceased members of the family together with keeping of vigils and memorials.

It is significant that several of the family with the name Heinrich (III, 25) achieved a particularly strong standing in the larger world of trade and politics. This Heinrich was the first to study abroad in Italy and obtain a Doctorate of Laws in Bologna. His achievement was striking in that he was recognized as having the privilege of being designated as ‘licentia magistrandi’, giving him administrative rights across the European-Roman lands. He apparently was committed to a spiritual career, serving with the Archbishop Walram in the City of Cologne as secretary and adviser. As indicated earlier, he spent many years as envoy to Pope Benedict XII in Avignon. Eventually these issues and negotiations involved King Ludwig of Bavaria as well as Edward the III of England. He was constantly representing the interests of Cologne and alternated much of his efforts between Avignon and Cologne. When Wilhelm von Gnepp succeeded Archbishop Walram, he chose his own confidant and secretary and so Heinrich became the legal adviser to Innocent VI, now pope in Avignon.

His most important task was to organize and secure the churches holdings and assets in all the significant cities loyal to the church. He maintained this role through the subsequent Pontificates of Urban V and Gregory XI. As a reward for his work, he was handsomely rewarded with what were termed benefices that included properties in many cities including Cologne, not to mention many lesser benefits for numerous relatives, illegitimate children and servants. Among those who secured lucrative incomes as clerics in the Dioceses of Cologne and Luettich were Arnold, Bertram, Albert, Hildebrand, Johann (V, 59-65); sons of his brother Johann, Arnold, Hildebrand, and Andreas (IV, 52-55); sons of Hildebrand, Johann and Heinrich; sons of his sister as well as those not determined in respect to their connection such as Wilhelm, Heinrich and Hermann (III,39-41). He demonstrated an exceptionally strong family concern and his position allowed him to help the family maintain its status as a significant patrician family.

Early on as the trade of the German Hanse flourished in the 14th Century, the Sudermanns did not hesitate to move beyond its local connections. Hildebrand (I, 14) was active in trade with Norway. Bertram (I, 19) was active in Riga where he secured stranded trade goods. In the second half of the 13th Century the City of Krakow, strategically located in the centre of Poland obtained rights to trade in the German Hanse, which brought in the first of the Krakow line of the family.

Hildebrand, the exceptionally strong representative in London had started the export of copper and other metals from Norway. He was given protection by King Edward I of England in 1307 when Norwegian pirates commandeered a loaded ship, which was located and ordered released by Edward I. He later left England, putting his brother Konrad (I, 15) in charge.

Hildebrand Sudermann (III, 28) took over the trade in England and actually established a home and family in

London. In 1323, Edward II gave him royal privileges, which put him on the same footing as English merchants in respect to tariffs and the right to trade across the land. These rights were maintained under Edward III as well as Richard II and continued to a large degree into the 16th Century for his successors. His strong areas of trade were the wool and fleece trade, the linens from Flanders, hides, barrels and wines.

The most significant and natural trade was with the Northwestern Low countries, Flanders and England. As early as 1266 they had access to the Cologne guildhall in London. In Bruges, it was considered the strongest trading partner as early as 1250. At that point, the Italians controlled the currency in England and had the strongest connections with the English monarchy. Johann Sudermann (IV, 58) was the active agent in Bruges. Between 1358 and 1388 there were constant struggles for privileges and trading rights between various partners and associates, which consumed a lot of the time of Johann Sudermann. In the year 1329, the merchants from Dortmund established a cooperative, together with merchants from the cities of Soest, Luebeck and Braunschweig, each established their Hanse Headquarters in Antwerp. They recognized the significance of Antwerp as a centre conducive to facilitating trade in the Northwestern region.

In 1337, Edward III, began the 100-year War with France. To punish Flanders, he transferred the lucrative English wool trade from Bruges to Antwerp. A very strong trade spearheaded by Heinrich together with Hildebrand (I, 14) in London ensued. But by 1339, the wool trade had moved back to Bruges. In just over three years, Heinrich had become very well off and remained as a well-regarded tradesman in Antwerp. Today, the street Rue Sudermann near the cathedral still reminds us of this Heinrich.

In 1338, Edward III landed in Antwerp with the express objective of forming a coalition with his brother in law, Ludwig of Bavaria, and several Dukes. Under Edward II, the treasury in England had been depleted and credit with the Italian Banks had been strained. The income from tariffs had also been depleted. He turned to the Sudermann family and several other trading families in Antwerp for credit which they extended to him for tariff free export privileges. The merchants had very little faith that the king would be able to pay his debt and required an insurance guarantee from the Italian banks. Thereafter, the family became active in providing more loans to the King for the right to export "without paying custom and subsidy thereon". This was a very favorable trade position. Unfortunately, by 1339, the King was unable to meet his obligations and so the Dukes and the King of Bavaria gave privileges to the merchant bankers to support the loans. These merchants remained the most reliable source of funds for the King and so the King maintained their privileges. These privileges resulted in a great deal of hostility from the English merchants, which often resulted in disputes and court hearings.

Hildebrand was able to maintain a very strong position of leadership of the Hanse Merchants in the London Guildhall. In 1351, they were able to obtain trading privileges for the import of fish, fish oil and other wares from Norway without tariff or custom duties. Similarly, they were able to import wine from the German states with the same exemptions.

However, a very strong anti-foreigner sentiment had arisen in England. In addition, the black plague came to England from Europe. These two factors had a very strong negative effect on the trade situation. The negative feelings erupted in violence. Several storage and trade facilities were attacked and several merchants and their staff were killed, both English and foreigners. Edward III, withdrew privileges and demanded damages. The situation between Flanders and England became very strained and the trade was severely affected. At the end of the day, 1351 was a very difficult year for Hildebrand, with accusations, threats, his goods seized and other restraints imposed.

In researching these materials, the port named Boston is frequently mentioned. This was a significant early port town on the east coast of England in Lincolnshire. The reason for the original development of the town was that it lay on the point where navigable tide- water was alongside the land route, which provided several points of connection with major land routes in England. During the eleventh and twelfth centuries, Boston grew into a notable town and port. The duty on merchant's imports was somewhat less than the duties charged to the merchants of London, which favored its trade. By the opening of the thirteenth century, it was already significant in trade with the continent of Europe and ranked as the port of the Hanseatic League. Much of Boston's trade at this time was in wool, and Boston is said by the locals to have been built on it. Later, when the wool trade began to decline in the fifteenth century as the industry shifted to the business of weaving cloth, the Hansa merchants quit the town and Boston's wealth declined.

When the city of Krakau was established in Poland, it was in effect a settlement of German merchants who were given the right of self-government by the Duke, which included the right to trade throughout the land of Poland with no tariffs or customs required of them. Heinrich Sudermann (I and II, 8) recognized the potential of iron as well as the large copper resources of that area. His name appears in 1302 as well as in 1309 and 1312 as council member of the city council. In addition, the major advantage of Krakau was its location as the major transit route for goods and staples. Furs, wines, copper and iron imported from Hungary and linens and other goods were exported to Hungary. This advantage allowed this city to develop and enrich the merchants who had the trade privileges, which included Heinrich Sudermann. He soon acquired considerable property in and around the city. Eventually, the political interventions and the resistance of the Polish people resulted in the erosion of the advantages the German merchants enjoyed. By 1320, he had lost most of his property. His sons, Hanko and Heinko (II, 22 and 23) continued to engage in city administration during the years 1338 to 1342. Subsequently, their influence and activity diminished and disappeared completely by 1370.

The story of the Sudermanns and their activity in the trade of the Hanse culminates and comes to an end to a large degree with the activity of the last of the Heinrich Sudermanns. This Heinrich (VI, 141) son of the Hermann in the picture located in Kimbell Art Museum in Fort Worth, Texas was in the seventh generation of this family.

His story from the year 1552 became the story of the endeavors of the Hanse in both the Europe and England. From 1552 to 1556 was the representative from Cologne on trade consultations and delegations, which required travel time, which added up to two years and twenty days during a four year period. In 1556 he received the appointment of Syndic for the Cities of the Hanse. He retained this position until his death in 1591. The English merchants had become increasingly dissatisfied with the privileges given to the linen trade controlled by the Cologne traders in Antwerp.

In England, the organization, Merchant Adventurers, was gaining strength and under Queen Elizabeth I, the longstanding privileges of the Hanseatic League were finally revoked. Prior to this event, continual efforts had been undertaken to establish alternate trade centers in such European ports such as Emden and Hamburg, as when the King of Spain, sovereign of the Low Countries, prohibited English ships from coming to the Low Countries. Heinrich's constant struggle with the English monarchs beginning with Mary, wife of King Philipp of Spain, to Elizabeth I, (who had the help of the notorious Walsingham) became more and more difficult. He had hoped a change from Mary to Elizabeth would improve his position. Disappointingly, the struggle with the expansionist and repressive policies toward the Hanseatic League by Elizabeth doomed the eventual outcome of his efforts. In addition, the merchants that were in charge of the activities in London, engaged in self-serving practices and abuses that contributed to the lack of success in negotiations with the Queen. With great disappointment to him, Heinrich's attempts in 1560 failed to reinstate the privileges.

The Polish/German Connection

Research in the Mennonite Encyclopedia carries some specific names and dates as to the Suderman's move from the Netherlands to Poland. As early as 1619, records show two brothers, Elias and Daniel Suderman from Holland registered as students in the Elbing Gymnasium (High School). Jacob Suderman, a Mennonite merchant, born in 1620 in Rotterdam came to Danzig sometime between 1660 and 1670. The prominent German author, Hermann Suderman is a descendant of this family, born in 1857. It is probable that various other Sudermans arrived and settled in Danzig and the Polish Werder in the sixteen hundreds. The encyclopedia states that the Suderman name was found in Elbing, Heubden, and Koenigsberg. From this area the name was transplanted to Russia.

In Holland, a Dutch Mennonite family was found in Rotterdam in the 17th and 18th Century. Of these Rotterdam Sudermans, who were all merchants, were old Flemish. Elyas Suderman was a deacon in the Old Flemish congregation from 1662, while others belonged to the Waterlander, a Mennonite church, and later to the United Rotterdam Mennonite Church.

Willem Suderman was a preacher in the Waterlander church from 1675-1700 as well as of the United Rotterdam Mennonite Church from 1700-1701. Jan Suderman, a deacon of the United Congregation from 1710 was in 1711, a representative of the Rotterdam congregation in the Dutch Committee for Foreign Needs. He also published a book defending the Mennonite position. According to Piet Visser, the Waterlander church in Amsterdam was one of the many Mennonite congregations in Holland.

Research in the Mennonite Encyclopedia and various other sources also indicate that in the 16th Century, some of the Sudermans moved from their Catholic tradition to embrace the Protestant expression of faith. A prominent poet and hymn writer, Daniel Suderman was born in Liege, France in 1550. He was a painter and engraver by profession. However, he was very committed to the mystical tradition and researched and published extensively on such well-known mystics as Eckhart, Bernhard of Clairvaux and others. One of his 435 hymns, "Elend mit shad, wer tugend hat" is included in his hymnal, a copy of the hymnal can be found in Goshen College.

This Daniel Suderman was also a follower of Kaspar Schwenckfeld. Within the first two decades of the 16th-century Reformation, there were Christians in Europe known as Lutherans, Zwinglians, Anabaptists and Schwenckfelders, followers of Kaspar Schwenckfeld. A few Schwenckfeld congregations exist today in Pennsylvania. Throughout history they have been known for their interest in education and learning, with extensive literary activity. In some areas the Anabaptists and Schwenkfelders were close as the Schwenckfelders often used Anabaptist writings. The Mennonites often came to their assistance in the Netherlands during persecutions and assisted them in their immigration to Pennsylvania.

In addition to his musical compositions, Daniel Suderman spent a great deal of his time and energy collecting, editing and printing spiritual texts. In 1613 he printed a publication

' Harmonia oder Concordantz' in which he set out objective and impartial information providing a comparison of the Catholic, Lutheran and Reformed Confessions with the objective of strengthening a common Christian understanding of faith.

The Kimbell Art Museum in Fort Worth, Texas, has, among its acquisitions, two oil-on-wood panels entitled, Hermann Sudermann, Burgomaster of Cologne, with his Sons and St Thomas, and, Elizabeth Hupp Sudermann with her Daughters and St Ursula, painted in the time period 1515 to 1530 by the artist Barthel Bruyn, the Elder, 1495-1555.

My brother, Henry Suderman, first saw this painting when he visited the Kimbell Museum in 1972. He had been transferred to Dallas, Texas by the Canadian Imperial Bank of Commerce in 1970 and was fortunate that the picture was on display at the time of his visit as he was told that it is often not on display. These pictures led him to engage in research in respect to the origins and activities of that particular Sudermann family. He obtained prints as well as photocopies of the notes contained in the section entitled, German, Sixteenth Century Art of the Museum research material. Here are some of the notes accompanying the picture:

Barthel Bruyn worked in Cologne from 1515 introducing there an important school of portrait painting that remained active long after his death. The style of painting he brought to Cologne was Netherlandish in character, reflecting Bruyn's early study with the Haarlem painter Jan Joest and the strong influence of his contemporary Joos van Cleve. Unlike most portrait painters of the period, such as Lucas Cranach and Hans Holbein, Bruyn had no connections with any court; his subjects and patrons were the burghers of Cologne, whom he portrayed with sympathy and understanding. He also painted numerous altarpieces, the donor portraits of which constitute an important category in his portrait oeuvre.

The Kimbell panels once formed part of such an altarpiece, the central panel of which is now missing; they depict members of the prominent Sudermann family of Cologne. The dark simple attire of the men is appropriately earnest and sober, in contrast to the livelier atmosphere of the feminine panel, evoked by the jewelry, the bright colors of the ornamented dress and the curving lines of the sweeping drapery. St Ursula, whose angel-supported mantle shelters the women, figures prominently in paintings of the Cologne area because it was there that she was martyred with her attendant virgins. St Thomas has no comparable ties to Cologne; when depicted in this panel, holding a carpenter's square, he is the patron of builders and architects, a reference perhaps to Hermann Sudermann's occupation or accomplishments.

Eventually, my brother Henry took a position with the Bank of British Columbia and was assigned to a position in London, England. Here he researched the archives in both London and Cologne. One of the sons in the picture is Heinrich Sudermann, who became the head of the Hanse Trading Organization that dominated trade in northern Europe and England during the 15th and 16th Century. An amazing discovery for my brother, Henry, was that Heinrich Sudermann was frequently in London during the 16th Century and had an office on the Thames not far from where Henry was stationed with the Bank of British Columbia. The archives in London have significant information on the trade and banking activities of the Hanse. The archives contain many copies of reports and memorandum in the handwriting of Heinrich Sudermann.

The strength of Bruyn's portrait art can be seen in the way he has capture convincing and unpretentious likenesses of specific individuals. Hermann and Elizabeth Sudermann are especially impressive in their pious air of bourgeois dignity, self-awareness and reserve. Such qualities frequently come through in Bruyn's work as he attempted to please his conservative patrons. Typical of his earlier work, the portraits of his male members of the family are more lifelike and varied than those of the females. Even among the very similar faces of the little girls, Bruyn has attempted to distinguish each by a slight difference of expression………

Cologne family men

Cologne family women

Sowing Winter Wheat

There is a sign erected near Hillsboro, Kansas by the Kansas State Historical Society and State Highway Commission with the following information:

TURKEY RED WHEAT

Children in Russia handpicked the first seeds of this famous winter wheat for Kansas. They belonged to the Mennonite Colonies preparing to emigrate from the steppes to the American prairies. A peace-loving sect, originally from Holland, the Mennonites had gone to the Crimea from Prussia in 1790 when Catherine the Great offered free lands, military exemption and religious freedom. They prospered until these privileges were threatened in 1871.

Three years later they immigrated to Kansas, where the Santa Fe R.R. offered thousands of acres on good terms in McPherson, Harvey, Marion and Reno Counties, and where the legislature passed a bill, which exempted religious objectors from military service. Within a month after landing in New York the Mennonites planted the red-gold grains their children had selected. The harvest was the first of the great crops of hard Turkey Red and its derivatives that have made Kansas the Granary of the Nation.

The Suderman family celebrated an extended family reunion in Kansas in 2011. Many of the ancestral Suderman family were part of this first wave of emigration from Russia to America and a genealogy book published by Carolyn (Suderman) Zeisset in 1975 had made the connection with the Suderman family descendants who had remained in Russia and immigrated to Canada in the 1920's following the Russian Revolution.

The first president of Bethel College in Newton, Kansas was Cornelius Wedel. It is very likely that there is a family connection with my maternal Wedel side of our family with some of the Wedels that came to Kansas. Unfortunately, little has been undertaken in respect to the delineation of the Wedel Family genealogy.

Each generation leaves a mark or an investment for the future. This is true economically as is reflected in the Turkey Red Wheat remembrance. We also leave legacies in many other ways. This acknowledgement of the contribution of the first Russian Mennonite in the USA is an economic legacy. We hopefully leave many other legacies in the form of institutions, family values, career enhancements, etc.

The first generation of immigrants is, of necessity, preoccupied with survival needs. In the case of the Mennonites immigrants who arrived in the 1920's, survival was made very difficult in that the depression in America arrived in 1929 and continued throughout the 1930's. In spite of the enormous financial restraints, basic institutions were established such as churches, Bible Schools and some Colleges. However, the impetus for charitable giving does not become strong until the second or third generation when wealth has been accumulated.

The following newsletter was prepared by my brother Henry in anticipation of a bus trip from Winnipeg to Kansas. The bus trip did not take place, instead individuals either drove or flew to Kansas for the reunion. The information is nonetheless relevant to describe the intentions of the reunion.

HENRY L SUDERMAN NEWSLETTER, DATED MARCH 31st, 2011

With memories still fresh for the wonderful time we had at Manitoba reunion, hosted by siblings Rita Menzies, Alvin Suderman, and Ruth Suderman, let's embark on a journey retracing the trail taken by relatives of the past.

You will recall our bus trip south of Winnipeg, when we saw where the first Mennonite settlers from Russia disembarked on the Red River and made their way east to what today is Steinbach, Manitoba. An attached picture shows the first Mennonite group arrived at the Niverville landing site on August 1, 1874. The plaque refers Jacob Y Schantz leading this group.

On pages 62 and 63 of Carolyn Zeisset's genealogy book, you will read about the Peter and Adelgunda Suderman Jost family, which was one of the pioneer families that came to Manitoba in 1874. In Toronto, Jacob Y Schantz met them on July 19, 1974, arriving in Manitoba in August. The Jost family could easily been in the very first group that arrived by boat up the Red River on August 1, 1874. There were no railroads in Manitoba at this time.

However, after spending one winter there and finding the cold weather too much to bear, the Jost family, having sufficient financial resources to move on, left with several other families for Marion County, near present day Hillsboro. Subsequently, this influenced Adelgunda's siblings, Maria Suderman Unruh, Helena Suderman Dyck, and Jacob

Suderman to move directly to Kansas from Russia with spouses and offspring.

Their mother, Adelgunda Penner Suderman Dueck, who is our great-great-great grandmother, came from Russia a year or two later and initially lived with the Jost family. Back in the 1970's, it fascinated both my father John P Suderman and me that a direct antecedent is buried in Kansas when we pieced the information together.

So why not follow this trail to Kansas. This first newsletter is simply to inform you of the planned event and get your reaction, suggestions, and interest in joining us.

In general, we can trace our heritage back five hundred years to the formation of Mennonites when Menno Simons, left the Catholic Church in the reformation to form the Mennonites. With oppression and political upheaval, our forefathers where never loath to stay put in circumstances in which they were not comfortable.

Of interest to all our Toews relatives who are most welcome to join us at this reunion is the sojourn in Alexanderwohl, Russia. My grandmother, Helena Toews Suderman, was born in Alexanderwohl in the 1880's. I'm curious, were my grandparents married in the church building shown on top of page 3. A decade before, the leading Mennonite church in this village uprooted lock stock and barrel, (apparently it had many members in adjoining villages and resettled in Kansas. Today it is still a thriving church in rural Kansas with an eye-catching structure on the main road between Newton and Hillsboro. The following is an excerpt from the church's web site:

History of Alexanderwohl

"The Immigrant House, our first American house of worship"

The origin of Alexanderwohl Church families can be traced back to the Netherlands in the 16th Century.

During the 1600-1650, many of these families migrated to West Prussia, settling in the Danzig area between the Vistula and Nogat Rivers.

The Przechowko church in West Prussia, which is the mother church of Alexanderwohl, was composed of Mennonites who settled near Schwetz on the Vistula River.

In 1820-21 a large portion of the Przechowko Church migrated to the Molotschna area in South Russia. During this journey they met Czar Alexander I, who wished them well ("wohl" in German), prompting the naming of the new village, Alexanderwohl, established in South Russia.

In 1874, Elder Jacob Buller led the entire Alexanderwohl church membership plus other families (about 800 persons) as they embarked on two ships, the Cimbria and Teutonia, to leave Russia.

A large portion of the group settled near what is now Goessel, Kansas.

The Santa Fe Railroad, which sold land to the Mennonites, built two immigrant houses near the middle of the section on which the church now stands. After families moved to newly built homes of their own, the immigrant houses were moved together to form a place of worship.

In 1886, a new church was completed on the present site.

The church building, originally built in the "Dutch Mennonite" style, underwent a major remodeling project in 1928. The education wing was added in 1961, and the north addition in 1983.

Today, Alexanderwohl has approximately 600 members and is affiliated with the General Conference and Western District Conference.

John 3:16 in Low German, more Dutch than German:

Dan Gott siene Leew to dise Welt wea soo groot, daut hee sienen eentsjen Sän jeef, daut aul dee, dee aun am gleewen, nich feloaren gonen, oba daut eewje Läwen haben.

- Jehaunes Kapetel 3:16

Alexanderwohl Mennonite Church, South Russia

We will be staying in the student residence on the Tabor College Campus in Hillsboro from Friday evening until Monday morning. Meals will be provided to us as a group in the college cafeteria. We will be fully occupied this weekend with visits to Museums (The Mennonite Settlement Museum, The Schaeffler Family House, details at http://www.hillsboro-museums.com/), Tabor College, particularly the Library that houses the Center for Mennonite Brethren Studies, http://www.tabor.edu/about-tabor/center-mennonite-brethren-studies, historical Mennonite churches and their cemeteries, and tours of early settlements of our kin from yesteryear. Details will be provided in future newsletters that will be sent regularly prior to the reunion in June of 2011.

When you leave Hillsboro, be sure you have ordered the great Hillsboro German sausage. People from all over the world come to Hillsboro to buy and ship Hillsboro's famous sausage back to their homes. Well, that's just a partial "taste" of Hillsboro. There will be many more memories to take with. Greater details to follow in further newsletters.

You will note that we are not waiting the customary five years between the reunions. Firstly, many of the regular attendees are getting advanced in age and each year delay reduces the number of who are physically able to attend. Further, the five-year stretch between reunions diminishes the memory of each that who attended previously. For those who happen to miss a reunion, the ten year gap is simply too long.

For those who wish to travel independently, you may of course plan your own itinerary. The closest airport is in Wichita, Kansas, just over an hour's drive south of Hillsboro.

PART TWO

The following is a copy of the Article on Mennonite Villages, which appeared in *The Hutchinson News* on June 5th, 2011. The article makes references to Karen (Suderman) Penner who is one of the many Suderman relatives from the Kansas area.

Villages were deep roots for Mennonites

Stone markers, tree rows, and cemeteries are County's remnants.

By Amy Bickel

Tall barren prairie lay in every direction the eye could see. Not a sound stirred, except for the wind amid the grasses and the insects that swarmed.

Jacob Wiebe and his family and a number of other Mennonites had traveled from southern Russia to the Kansas plains where they sought religious freedom among the other pioneers just settling in the nearby fifteen-year-old state. They had decided to leave the green fields of the Crimea forever, hearing that Kansas had similar soils to their native country – a good place to grow wheat. The group purchased a tract of land in central Kansas from the Santa Fe Railroad.

And amid a hot August sun in 1874, Wiebe and congregation leaders traveled the uninhabited landscape fourteen miles from Peabody to an area of Marion County.

We rode in the deer grass to the little stake that marked the spot I had chosen. When we reached the spot, I stopped. My wife asked me, 'Why do you stop?' I said. 'We are going to live here.' Then she began to weep.

Wiebe wrote the story as part of an essay forty years later. For the women, it must have seemed daunting to begin building a home on the lonely landscape – far from her native homeland, far from any settlement, said area Karen Penner as she read the marker that tells Wiebe's tale of settling the plains in 1874.

It must have been overwhelming Penner said yet these settlers had optimism for their future. They named it, their new home, Gnadenau, or Meadow of Grace.

Gnadenau was only the forefront of a large number of Mennonite settlements in south-central Kansas nearly a hundred and forty years ago – ghost villages now only marked by stone markers, tree rows and cemeteries.

They had first migrated from Europe to Russia under Catherine the Great for religious freedom. Nevertheless, one hundred years later, changes took place under Alexander II that impacted their beliefs, including a universal military service act that would require the peaceful group to fight.

Thus, by the end of 1874, the first arrival of Mennonites, roughly 1,900 people, settled an area that consisted of 60,000 acres of land in Marion, McPherson, Harvey and Reno counties, according to a June 1973 article in Mennonite Life. And some of the hard winter wheat that made Kansas the breadbasket of the nation reached that states in the baggage of the German-speaking immigrants form the steppes of southern Russia.

At first, the settlers were determined to retain the village tradition and pattern of farmland distribution they had had in Russia, according to the publication. Penner said that each town was set up like these Russian villages, with long streets with several small farmsteads spaced evenly apart in a row along the street. Typically, in the middle of this long block was a school. Some villages also had a gristmill for processing the wheat the families brought with them. Each farmstead was given nearby land to tend.

Gnadenau was just the first of more than a dozen villages settled in Marion and surrounding counties. It also was the largest, the new home of 34 families, or 164 people. A church was built, then a store and a couple of blacksmith shops. A large gristmill was built just west of the village and operated by Jacob Friesen and his son, the publication stated.

Other communities had ethnic names like Schoenthal or Fair Valley in English; Gruenfeld pr Greenfield; and

Hoffnungsthal, which means Hope Valley. The area was divided into two communities, in essence, the Alexanderwohl and Krimmer Mennonite communities, according to the Mennonite publication. The Alexanderwohl community was the largest and consisted of eight villages in all.

These early pioneers tried the village setup for just three years before it was abandoned – due to confusion in paying taxes and because families wanted personal property and independence, according to the publication. The Gnadenau village, however, lasted several more years before it became a ghost village.

"With the American system of private landownership, some moved out of the village sooner", said Peggy Goertzen, director of the Center of Mennonite Studies at tabor College in Hillsboro. However, she said, "You can still see village locations, and at Hochfeld, you can still see the village pattern.

On a recent spring day, Penner, a historian and board member with Newton's Bernhard Warkentin House – the man that helped bring many Mennonites to Kansas – toured many of the former village sites. A large green sign marks Hochfeld, where trees still mark the outline of the village. A mile to the north lays Springfield, which is also marked by a sign and a cemetery. At Alexanderfeld, there is a cemetery, as well as a church, school and stone pillar.

Then there is the first site of Gnadenau, where a stone still marks the spot where a cemetery once was located. Penner said most of the graves, as well as the church, were moved west to another site. That church burned down several years ago and a new one was built in Hillsboro. Hillsboro has a full sized replica of the wind-powered gristmill built in 1876 at the Gnadenau display.

Penner grew up around the Ebenfeld Mennonite Brethren church area in Marion County, near the town of Auline. This weekend she and her family gathered for a reunion at Bethel College, which included talking about their roots.

She said her family also plans to install a gravestone for her great grandmother, Adelgunda Penner Suderman Dueck, who died in 1888. She was buried with a couple of family members near the Alexanderfeld community – a common practice back then. The family moved the grave to the Gnadenau cemetery in the 1970's but never put a marker on the plot, she said. The family is beginning to raise money to mark her grave. Family, after all, she said, is important.

"There is a saying that, for your children to have wings, they must have roots," she said "And to know where you are going in life, you must know from where you came. That is my philosophy. I just like to learn the stories of who these people were, what they went through. That is what it makes it fun for me – finding they were real people not just a name and a date."

A sign is staked at each end of Hochfeld, a community settled around 1874. The tree rows from when it was an active village are still visible. Villages lasted about three years before residents dispersed to their own farms.

PART THREE

The Gravestone

Here is the new gravestone of Adelgunda Penner Suderman Dueck (1805- 1888), my great, great, great grandmother, placed in October of 2011. Adelgunda added the name Dueck when she married Klaas Dueck in 1842. Heinrich Suderman lived from 1806 to 1842.

Here is a poem written by Elmer F. Suderman, grandson of Adelgunda.

Memories Of A Mennonite Father

To walk into sunset
through a wheat field
with my Mennonite father-
silence, sky, sun, June wind
encircling us-
was to see memories move
within his eyes,
to hear the heart's ear
the silent strong tenor
of his soil's past.

Elmer F. Suderman

The Friesen family August 2012.

About the Author

Erna Friesen received her education in public schools and the Mennonite Educational Institute. She obtained a Bachelor of Arts Degree at UBC. She taught in elementary as well as in High School for seven years, and then took fourteen years to be a mother and home maker. In her early forties, she entered Law School at UBC, and with Harold Epp founded the firm of Friesen & Epp. Erna has been active as a lawyer and engaged in her community. Together with a small group she was instrumental in the founding of the Menno Simons Centre as well as The Point Grey Inter-Mennonite Fellowship in Vancouver. She served as board member and chair of Regent College and board member of Canadian Mennonite University in Winnipeg and has been active on the board of the Faith and Learning Society in establishing Peace Studies at the University of the Fraser Valley. With her husband, John Friesen, professor at UBC she now enjoys retirement with her children and their families in Vancouver, Whistler, Maui and Palm Desert.